Cinderella

A Pantomime

John Crocker
with lyrics by Eric Gilder

Samuel French – London
New York – Sydney – Toronto – Hollywood

MADE AND PRINTED IN GREAT BRITAIN BY
LATIMER TREND & COMPANY LTD PLYMOUTH
MADE IN ENGLAND

CHARACTERS

DANDINI

LITTLE MISS MUFFET

PRINCE CHARMING

BARON HARDUP

BUTTONS

CINDERELLA

TUTTI }
FRUTTI }   The Ugly Sisters

DOBBIN   A horse

FAIRY GODMOTHER

RAG)
TAG)   The Broker's Men
BOBTAIL)

THE KING

A BEAR

CHORUS as Inn servants and maids, Huntsmen, Hounds, Fairies,
     Courtiers, Glee Singers, etc.

SYNOPSIS OF SCENES

PART ONE

SCENE 1   THE ROYAL FOREST
SCENE 2   A VILLAGE STREET
SCENE 3   THE KITCHEN AT HARDUP HALL
SCENE 4   OUTSIDE HARDUP HALL
SCENE 5   THE UGLY SISTERS BOUDOIR
SCENE 6   THE SERVANTS HALL AT THE PALACE
SCENE 7   THE KITCHEN AT HARDUP HALL

PART TWO

SCENE 8   THE PALACE BALLROOM
SCENE 9   A FOREST GLADE
SCENE 10   THE MUSIC ROOM AT HARDUP HALL
SCENE 11   OLD BOYS REUNION
SCENE 12   THE ROYAL WEDDING RECEPTION

Running time approximately two hours and thirty minutes.

PRODUCTION NOTE

Pantomime, as we know it today, is a form of entertainment all on its own, derived from a number of different sources - the commedia dell' arte, (and all that that derived from), the ballet, the opera, the music hall, and the realms of folk-lore and fairy tale. And elements of all of these are still to be found in it. This strange mixture has created a splendid topsy-turvy world where men are women, women are men, where the present is embraced within the past, where people are hit but not hurt, where authority is constantly flouted, where fun is poked at everything including pantomime itself at times, and, above all, where magic abounds and dreams invariably come true. In other words, it is - or should be - fun. Fun to do and fun to watch and the sense of enjoyment which can be conveyed by a cast is very important to the enjoyment of the audience.

Pantomime can be very simply staged if resources are limited. Basically a tab surround at the back, tab legs at the sides and a set of traverse tabs for the frontcloth scenes, together with the simplest of small cut-out pieces to suggest the various locales, (or even just placards with this information written on them) will suffice. Conversely, there is no limit to the extent to which more lavish facilities can be employed.

The directions I have given in the text adopt a middle course and are based on a permanent setting of a cyclorama skycloth at the back. About two thirds of the depth downstage is a false proscenium, immediately behind which are the lines for a set of traverse tabs. Below the false proscenium are arched entrances left and right, with possibly one foot reveals to the proscenium. A border will be necessary at some point between the false proscenium and the cyclorama to mask lighting battens and the top of the cyclorama. For Part II a rostrum about two feet high is introduced which is set a few feet or so in front of the cyclorama and runs the width of the stage. Lastly there is a set of steps leading from the front of the stage into the auditorium, which I have referred to as the catwalk. I have imagined it to be set stage left, but it is unimportant whether it is left or right.

Into this permanent setting are placed various wings left and right, (I have catered for one a side set on a level with the border, but a greater depth of stage may require two a side for masking purposes). Cut-out ground rows set in front of the cyclorama, or on the rostrum complete the full sets. On smaller stages these cut-outs seen against the cyclorama give a better impression of depth than backcloths. The frontcloth fly lines come in behind the traverse tabs. Cloths can, of course be tumbled or rolled if flying space is limited. It is a good tip always to bring in the traverse tabs when a cloth has to be lowered, then if any hitch occurs the lights can still come up and the actors get on with the scene. Similarly, I have indicated where the traverse tabs should be closed in frontcloth scenes so that there is plenty of time for the cloth to be flown before the end of the scene. The quick flow of one scene into the next is important if a smooth running production is to be achieved.

Sometimes the action escapes from the stage into the audience. Where this happens I have assumed an auditorium with aisles running the length of each side and transverse aisles at the front and about half way along its length. I have also assumed exits on each side and at the back of the auditorium, joined by passages out of sight of the audience, with a pass door from the stage into such a passage. These sequences will obviously have to be re-arranged to suit the auditorium used.

The settings and costumes should preferably be in clear bright colours to give a story book effect. It is probably best to try to have one overall period, but which period is immaterial. Also, of course, deliberate anachronisms should be introduced into some settings and some of the comics' costumes. Animal skins can be hired from Theatre-Zoo, 28 New Row, W.C.2.

Pantomime requires many props and often they will have to be home made. Instructions are given in the prop plot about any of the more awkward seeming ones. Props should also be colourfully painted and in pantomime most props should be much larger than reality. It is also wise for the property master to examine carefully the practical use to which a prop is to be put - it is very painful to be hit with a Giant's club of solid wood, one of material filled with foam plastic is far gentler!

I have not attempted to give a lighting plot as this entirely depends on the equipment available, but, generally speaking, most pantomime lighting needs to be full up, warm and bright. Pinks and ambers are probably best for this, but a circuit of blues in the cyclorama battens will help nightfall and dawn rising effects.

Follow spots are a great help for this kind of show, but not essential. But, if they are available, it is often effective in romantic numbers to fade out the stage lighting and hold the principals in the follow spots, quickly fading up on the last few bars because this can help to increase the applause! They can also be used for the Fairy and Demon to give them greater freedom of movement than with fixed front of house, or spot-bar spots.

Flash boxes, with the necessary colour and flash powders, and the maroon in Scene 5 can be obtained from the usual stage electrical suppliers and so can ultra violet equipment if it is used in Scene 7. For the transformation all the scenery, furniture, props - including the Fairy's wand - the costumes of the Fairy and Chorus will need to be treated with the special paint which shows up in the U.V. light.

The music has been specially composed so that it is easy for the less musically accomplished to master, but it is also scored in parts for the more ambitious. If an orchestra is available well and good, but a single piano will suffice. It is an advantage, however, if there can be a drummer as well. Not only because a rhythm accompaniment enhances the numbers, but also because for some reason never yet fully fathomed slapstick hits and falls are always twice as funny if they coincide with a well timed bonk on a drum, wood-block or whatever is found to make the noise best suited to the action. A drummer can also cope with the "whizzes" noted in the directions, though if necessary they can, of course, be done offstage. A special type of whistle can be got for this effect.

Pantomime demands a particular style of playing and production. The acting must be larger than life, but still sincere, with a good deal of sparkle and attack. Much of it must be projected directly at the audience, since one of pantomime's great advantages is that it deliberately breaks down the "fourth wall". The actors can literally and metaphorically shake hands with their audience who become almost another member of the cast; indeed, their active participation from time to time is essential. A word of warning, though, on this - the actors must always remain in control; for instance, if a Demon or villain encourages hissing he must be sure it is never to such an extent that he can no longer be heard. The producer should see that the story line is clearly brought out and treated with respect. There is always room for local gags and topical quips in pantomime, but they should not be overdone. Most important of all, the comedy, as any comedy, must never appear to be conscious of its own funniness.

Characterisation should be very clear and definite. I prefer the traditional use of a man to play the Dame and a girl to play the Principal Boy. In the case of the Dame, anyway, there is a sound argument for this - audiences will laugh more readily at a man impersonating a woman involved in the mock cruelties of slapstick than at a real woman. For this reason an actor playing a Dame should never quite let us forget he is a man, while giving a sincere character performance of a woman; further, he can be as feminine as he likes, but never effeminate. Tutti and Frutti should have some of that true sisterly spirit of bickering camaraderie which divides them amongst themselves but unites them against others. Their awareness of their ugliness, albeit unacknowledged, tends to make them cruel and selfish, by way of compensation. Luckily, they are also ridiculous which saves us from thoroughly disliking them.

A Principal Boy also requires a character performance, but, of course, with the implications reversed! An occasional slap of the thigh is not sufficient. Prince Charming should be thought of as an intelligent, amusing young man. His pose as his own valet tickles his sense of humour and his relationship with Dandini is a very easy informal one.

Dandini is, of course, the second Boy and should be played rather as a light comedian. He is very gay and impudent but he is also an efficient and loyal servant.

Principal Girls can be a bore, but only if they are presented as mere pretty symbols of feminine sweetness. Cinderella must not feel too sorry for herself. Fortunately she asks for little from life and has the virtue of enjoying what little she gets. Her nature is tender and kind, which is brought out in her relationship with Buttons, of whom she is genuinely fond.

Buttons' feeling for her is more than mere fondness, it is a deep protective love, but in his heart of hearts he realises it is unreciprocated. However, his sense of humour saves him from being too depressed by this. It also gives him an equanimity which enables him to come out on top of any awkward situation in which he finds himself.

Although Rag, Tag and Bobtail have three very different characters, they must work together very much as a team. Rag is the undisputed leader and always knows what should be done, it is how to achieve it which baffles him. Tag is a confirmed pessimist. He is certain that whatever they do is doomed to failure, anyway. Bobtail has the simple straightforward mind of a child and is quite unconcerned either with failure or success.

The Baron is rather muddle-headed. His life is spent in trying to keep up the appearances he knows are no longer there to be kept up.

Miss Muffet also has a conflicting nature. Really she is a trifle dizzy and not at all the strong-minded creature she tries to make herself out to be.

The King is not at all confused. He has a one-track mind and life outside the world of unsung songs has little meaning for him.

The Fairy Godmother is also very sure of her own mind and should be played as a benevolent immortal of great authority.

In the animal kingdom Dobbin is docile when it suits him and obstreperous when it does not. The Bear is a lumbering animal, perhaps with somewhat strange appetites for a bear, but not without charm.

I have made provision for a Chorus of six, but naturally the number used will vary according to how many are available.

John Crocker.

MUSIC 1. OVERTURE.

PART ONE

Scene One. THE ROYAL FOREST

(Fullset. Cut-out of trees along back. Forest wing L. Inn Piece R, with door in C, a window either side of door and a bench under each window. Inn sign - "THE TUFFET & SPIDER" hangs out from Inn. A long-handled broom rests by Inn door. Large flower-pot set in front of R. side of pros arch. Kindling wood sticks scattered L.)

(CHORUS, as Maids and Servants of the Inn, discovered singing and dancing)

MUSIC 2. Opening Chorus.

CHORUS: The year's in the Spring, the day's at the morn,
As somebody said before we were born;
And though the poet's dead and gorn
His words are true today.

(Enter DANDINI U. R.)

DANDINI: To lie in bed's a real disgrace,
So show a shining morning face.
The Prince is coming for the chase,
Shout out "Hip Hip Hooray!"

ALL: His retinue of ninety-three
Will hunt a rabbit for his tea.
So yoicks, tallyho, we say;
Full steam ahead and chocks away.
A-hunting, hunting we will go,
With stirrup-cups of cococo.
It's "Giddyup" and never "Whoa",
On this our hunting holiday.

DANDINI: Well now, my master the Prince will be here soon. Is all ready for the hunt breakfast?

CHORUS: Yes, Master Dandini.

1st CH: We've roasted a whole ox.

2nd CH: Broiled three sucking pigs.

3rd CH: And soused a hundred herrings.

DANDINI: Splendid, and talking of sousing, what's in the Stirrup Cup this year?

4th CH: Curds and whey.

DANDINI: Curds and whey! What's the use of curds and whey to a lot of thirsty hunters? They want beer. I'll have to see the Landlord about this. (calling into Inn) Landlord! Landlord!

(MUSIC 3. Enter LITTLE MISS MUFFET from Inn. She is very pretty, but very serious)

MUFFET: Yes? Did you want me?

DANDINI: Well - er - later, perhaps. At the moment I want the Landlord. Do you know where he is?

MUFFET: He isn't.

DANDINI: He isn't what?

MUFFET: He isn't a he, he's a she and she's me.

DANDINI: I see. Or do I? You don't look like old Landlord Muffet to me.

MUFFET: I am Miss Muffet, his niece. My uncle has retired and left me in charge of the Inn. I don't really like it though. I don't approve of strong drink; so in future we shall serve only draught milk and bottled yoghourt.

DANDINI: But - but the "Tuffet and Spider" is famous for its cellar, you'll ruin its good name.

MUFFET: Oh, I shall change that too. "The Tuffet and Spider" reminds me of a rather unfortunate incident in my life. I'm going to call it "The Jolly Junket", instead. Do you like junket?

DANDINI: Not much.

MUFFET: Well, I'm sure you'd like mine. It's so delicious and refreshing.

DANDINI: So are your lips.

MUFFET: I don't quite follow. How can my lips be delicious and refreshing?

DANDINI: Like this.

(He tries to kiss her, she slaps his face)

Ah, a wench with spirit! But the prize is worth the penalty.

(He tries to kiss her again and she again slaps his face)

Or is it? Miss Muffet, do you know who it is you're knocking about?

MUFFET: No.

DANDINI: (very grandly) I am Master Dandini, valet to His Royal Highness, Prince Charming. (slight pause) Well, doesn't that impress you?

MUFFET: Not at all.

DANDINI: But of course, if I was the Prince himself, it would.

MUFFET: Of course.

DANDINI: Ah, then give me a kiss and I'll tell you a secret.

MUFFET: Certainly not. I don't approve of kissing. That is - well, tell me the secret first and I'll see if it's worth a kiss.

DANDINI: (moving to her) No, first the kiss.

MUFFET: (backing towards Inn) No, first the secret.

DANDINI: The kiss.

MUFFET: The secret.

(They disappear into Inn)

5th CH: (looking off U.R.) Miss Muffet, here comes the Prince!

(MUSIC 4.)

CHORUS: The Prince! Here comes the Prince! Hurrah! Hurrah!

(PRINCE CHARMING enters U.R.)

PRINCE: I thank you, good people, for this loyal welcome. Now where is that knavish fellow Dandini? He said he would meet me here.

6th CH: Here he comes now, your Highness.

(DANDINI chases on MISS MUFFET from Inn. They do not see the PRINCE)

DANDINI: All right, Miss Muffet, you win - the secret first. But I shall expect a very big kiss after such a long chase.

MUFFET: And I shall expect a very big secret. What is it?

DANDINI: This - I am not really Dandini. I am the Prince disguised as Dandini.

(PRINCE looks surprised. CHORUS laugh)

PRINCE: Dandini!

DANDINI: (whirling round) Sir!

PRINCE: So you are the Prince?

DANDINI: Yes, sir - I mean, no, sir.

PRINCE: Then I must be Dandini.

DANDINI: No, sir - I mean, yes, sir.

PRINCE: Madam, I can see that his Royal Highness has something he wishes to say to his humble servant, Dandini. Perhaps you would leave us.

MUFFET: Certainly. (to CHORUS, claps hands) Let us continue our preparations for the hunt breakfast.

(CHORUS bow and bob curtsies to PRINCE and exit R.)

(starting to curtsey to PRINCE) Your high - (starting to curtsey to DANDINI) Your high - (curtsies) Your highnesses. (exits into Inn)

PRINCE: Dandini, what does this mean?

DANDINI: Well, sir, it was just a little game.

PRINCE: I'd say it was just plain flirting. But it's given me an idea. Dandini, you know that my father is giving a ball at the Palace tomorrow night so that I can choose a bride.

DANDINI: Do I not, sir? I have to issue invitations to every lady in the land. I'll be worn out.

PRINCE: No, you won't, because I shall deliver them for you. That's my idea. You want to be a Prince, Dandini, and so you shall - until the night of the ball.

DANDINI: Sir!

PRINCE: And I - I shall be the most impudent, roguish valet that lives - Master Dandini!

DANDINI: But this is wonderful, sir.

PRINCE: Then up to the palace with you, your Highness. Master Dandini will follow in a little while and we'll change clothes.

DANDINI: Certainly, sir. I mean - certainly, my man. And hurry up, fellow. We don't like to be kept waiting, you know.

(PRINCE bows with mock humility, which DANDINI condescendingly acknowledges and exits U. R.)

PRINCE: So for a time I am a free man - free to go where I like, say what I please and meet whom I choose; free even to fall in love. And who knows - perhaps I shall.

MUSIC 5. "I'LL FIND LOVE"

> I want to live like real folk,
>   Doing what real folk do,
> Pleasing myself what I do,
>   Like people like you.
> I want to walk in freedom,
>   Take any road I please,
> Over the tallest mountains
>   To far distant seas.
> Nothing to lose,
> Meet whom I choose,
>   See what I want to see.
> In someone's face,
> In some far place,
>   I'll find my destiny.
> Wonderful earth below me,
>   Infinite skies above.
> When ev'ry road I've travelled,
> When there's no more to show me,
> When ev'ry skein's unravelled -
>   Then I'll find love.

(under music) It's all very well being a Prince, with people bowing respectfully every time they see me, and lots of servants making sure my every whim is satisfied; but they seem to forget that I am a man too, and want to live a man's life.

> Nothing to lose, etc.

(At end of number PRINCE exits U. R. MUSIC 6. Loud hooting heard off L & BARON HARDUP enters L, dressed in an old and patched hunting kit and seated on a four-wheel scooter with large "L" plates, which is propelled by BUTTONS, who upsets scooter and BARON topples off)

BARON: Oh, Buttons, do be more careful. You'll never pass your test like that.

BUTTONS: (helping BARON up) Sorry, Baron. Still that's only the fifth spill in the last half mile.

BARON: Only! Just look at my hunting kit - ruined! And I wanted to look my best at the hunt today. I want to introduce my step-daughter gels to the Prince and see if I can't marry one of them off.

BUTTONS: Those two old frumps! Not a chance, Baron.

BARON: Well, I shall have to try. I'm expecting the Broker's Men daily and I must get some money from somewhere. Have you any money, Buttons?

BUTTONS: (holding up a 50p piece) Only this fifty pence piece.

BARON: (takes coin. Emotionally) Thank you, my boy, I shall remember this.

BUTTONS: (less emotionally, taking out notebook and making note) So shall I.

BARON: I shall now fortify myself for the rigours of the hunt with a drop of breakfast.

BUTTONS: A pint-sized drop?

BARON: No, no, moderation in all things. A two pint-sized drop. (exit into Inn)

BUTTONS: I don't think I came off very well there.

(BARON rushes out of Inn)

BARON: Ugh! Help! I've been poisoned!

BUTTONS: Poisoned?

BARON: Yes, I was given milk. That's all they've got there now - milk! Nasty thin, watery milk!

BUTTONS: Thin? Well, that's all right. All you've got to do is tell 'em you don't like milk thin.

BARON: Why?

BUTTONS: Because then they'll give you milk stout.

BARON: Brilliant! (exit into Inn)

BUTTONS: Oh dear, I did want that fifty pence. I was going to buy a present for Cinders with it. Cinders is my name for Cinderella. She's the Baron's real daughter, but she's very badly treated by her

BUTTONS: (continued) ugly step-sisters and I think it's a shame because she's awfully nice and very pretty and I love her very much. I haven't been able to tell her that yet, but I will someday - only I get so shy and -

(MUSIC 7. CINDERELLA is heard singing off R)

Why, here she comes now. I'll hide and surprise her. (hides behind woodwing L)

(CINDERELLA enters U.R.)

(poking head out) Cinders!

CINDERS: Hullo, Buttons. What are you doing?

BUTTONS: I'm hiding.

CINDERS: Well, you're not hiding very well. I can see you quite clearly.

BUTTONS: Can you? Well I never. (comes on holding something behind his back) I've got a present for you, Cinders.

CINDERS: A present? Oh, how lovely!

BUTTONS: (shyly, holds out a very battered dandelion) Yes, it is lovely, isn't it?

CINDERS: (not so sure) Oh, yes - very nice.

BUTTONS: I had a terrible fight to get it - with a rabbit. He was stronger than me, of course, but I beat him in the end.

CINDERS: Well, it was very sweet of you, Buttons. Thank you.

(Kisses him. He remains stock-still for a moment with a seraphic expression on his face, then begins to sway and falls over. CINDER- ELLA kneels beside him, worried)

Buttons, what's the matter? Are you ill?

BUTTONS: (coming-to, rather dreamily) Cinders! She kissed me! She kissed me! (rises shakily. MUSIC 8. Begins to do a little dance, eventually getting hold of broom by Inn) Dear Cinders. How beau- tiful you are. Kiss me again. (kisses broom and comes to with a start) Ow!

CINDERS: Buttons, there's a clock on this dandelion. Let's see what the time is. (blowing) One - two - three - four - five. Five o'clock already.

BUTTONS: Is it? I tell you what, Cinders, I'm going to plant one of these dandelion seeds. Oh, what a bit of luck - there's a flower pot. (puts seed in pot R of pros arch) There. I expect it'll grow very soon. (nothing happens, raising voice) I said, I expect it'll grow very soon)

(Dandelion flower shoots out of pot. MUSIC whizz)

Ooh! That's better. When it's fully grown I'll pick it for you.

CINDERS: But suppose somebody else takes it first?

BUTTONS: Oh dear, yes. I know - I'll ask all these people to look after it. (to AUDIENCE) I say, would you do that for us? Just keep an eye on the dandelion and if anybody tries to take it you shout "Buttons!" and I'll come and stop them. Let's try it, shall we? I'll go away and Cinderella will pretend to try and steal it and then you shout "Buttons!" as loud as you can. Right, stand by. (runs off R)

(CINDERELLA makes an elaborate show of pretending to steal dandelion)

(popping head back) Have you shouted yet? ... Well, I didn't hear you. Try again a bit louder. (disappears while they shout then pops head back again) That's better, but you know I might be a long way away so try once more just as loud as you can. (disappears again while they shout, then walks onstage) Ah, that's more like it, now we know it'll be quite safe.

CINDERS: I must go now, Buttons. I have to collect some kindling wood in the forest.

BUTTONS: Come on then, I'll help you. There's something I want to tell you.

(They start to walk L)

You see, Cinders, I lo-

BARON: (off in Inn, calling) Buttons! Buttons! I want you!

BUTTONS: Oh dear. (moving backwards to Inn, looking at CINDERELLA) I suppose I'd better go, Cinders. I don't really want to, though.

CINDERS: Never mind, Buttons, I shall see you again soon.

BUTTONS: Yes, I shall look forward to that. (reaches Inn door)

BARON: (opening Inn door) BUTTONS!

(BUTTONS is knocked onto his face and rises rubbing his nose)

BUTTONS: Ow! Pity I wasn't looking forward then.

(Exit BARON and BUTTONS into Inn)

CINDERS: Poor Buttons. Well, as he can't come with me, I shall have to dream up somebody else.

MUSIC 9. "I'LL HAVE TO DREAM UP SOMEBODY ELSE"

When somebody's a nobody and no-one wants to
know,
And nobody takes anybody where one wants to go,
Then someone must do something - because
someone isn't slow -
I'll have to dream up somebody else
I think perhaps a scientist, a person with a mission.
I'd live in his laborat'ry and better my position.

CINDERS: (continued)

But he <u>might</u> be just experimenting in atomic
        fission.
I'll have to dream up somebody else.
I should do something serious about it
And shake myself and get out of the rut.
I think that I'm terrific - but I doubt it,
I'm the girl to set the best men dreaming, but -
One can't make oneself glamorous when one's
        completely stony,
And though men say that advertising's just so
        much balony
I look exactly like the twin who hasn't had the
        Toni!
I'll have to dream up somebody else.
I'd like to sweep into the Ritz on one enchanted
        day
With Mr Norman Hartnell to escort me - and to
        pay.
But the dress that I am wearing is marked,
        "Reject - C & A"!
I'll have to dream up somebody else,
I'd like to meet a singing star, who's made a
        super platter,
With lots of charm, and lots of cars, and lots
        of dough to scatter,
But then he's got his flip side, so ... oh well,
        it doesn't matter
I'll have to dream up somebody else.
I might succumb to some great lover's passion
And give my all, and married life begin -
But soon I'd find my little nose had ash on -
And that is just the place where I came in!
Each time I dream up somebody there's some-
        thing sort of wrong,
For either he weighs twenty stone or else is four
        feet long,
And I've wasted five whole minutes while I've sung
        this little song -
And I haven't dreamed up anyone else!

(Exit CINDERELLA L.)

TUTTI: (off R.) Come on, Dobbin, get a gee-up on.

(MUSIC 10. Enter U.R. TUTTI pulling DOBBIN on by his bridle and
FRUTTI seated the wrong way round on DOBBIN. They are dressed in
grotesque riding habits)

FRUTTI: (as they enter) A-hunting we'll never go at this rate.

(DOBBIN stops in C.)

Oh dear, my end's stopped, Tutti.

TUTTI: So's mine, Frutti. Are you feeling all right, Dobbin?

(DOBBIN nods)

FRUTTI: Aren't you going to go any further?

(DOBBIN shakes tail)

TUT & FRU: Well, we'll have to see about that, won't we?

(DOBBIN nods head and tail and suddenly topples FRUTTI off and sits on her)

FRUTTI: Ow! Help! Get off! (she extricates herself) Really, Dobbin, how could you? Oh dear, we'll never get to the hunt today.

TUTTI: No, Pa said to meet him at the Tuffet and Spider and here we are miles from anywhere.

(DOBBIN waves a hoof at the Inn)

TUTTI: I think Dobbin wants to go and see a horse about a man. (bends her head towards him)

(DOBBIN impatiently shakes head and pushes TUTTI's head round so that she sees Inn)

Oh, I see. Frutti, we're there.

FRUTTI: Where?

TUTTI: Here.

FRUTTI: Where's here?

TUTTI: There.

FRUTTI: Where's there?

TUTTI: Here.

FRUTTI: Look, are we here or are we there?

TUTTI: Yes.

FRUTTI: WHERE?

TUTTI: At the Tuffet and Spider. (points) Look!

FRUTTI: (looks) Well, why didn't you say so?

TUTTI: AAAHHH!

(DOBBIN shakes head pityingly)

FRUTTI: Ooh, look! A dandelion.

TUTTI: Oh, yes, let's take it.

(They move to do so, followed interestedly by DOBBIN. AUDIENCE shout. TUTTI and FRUTTI jump back very startled knocking down DOBBIN and all fall in a heap. BUTTONS runs on from Inn)

BUTTONS: Somebody trying to take my dandelion? Ah, thank you.

FRUTTI: Oh, Buttons, we've just had such a shock. A lot of people shouted at us.

BUTTONS: Really?

TUTTI: Yes, help us up, Buttons, and then take Dobbin and get him some oats.

(DOBBIN reacts enthusiastically)

BUTTONS: (helping them up) Righto, there you are then. Now, come on, Dob -

(DOBBIN in his enthusiasm starts to go through Inn door)

(pulling him back by tail) Hey, wait! Not that way. Round the back. (he pulls DOBBIN off above Inn)

TUTTI: I wonder why all those people shouted at us?

FRUTTI: I can't think. Still, I don't expect they'll do it again. Let's take that dandelion.

(They move to dandelion. AUDIENCE shout. BUTTONS enters above Inn seated on DOBBIN, who runs up to TUTTI and FRUTTI, kicks them over then turns and runs off again)

TUT & FRU: OW!

BUTTONS: (as they go) Thank you.

TUTTI: What hit us?

FRUTTI: (rising, rubbing her bottom) I don't know, but it was a severe blow to my dignity.

TUTTI: (rising) But why do they keep shouting at us?

FRUTTI: I know, they want us to introduce ourselves.

TUTTI: Ah yes, of course. Well, how do you do? I'm Tutti, the pretty one -

FRUTTI: What!

TUTTI: And she's Frutti the - well, you can see for yourselves.

FRUTTI: Please pay no attention to my sister. She's just jealous of my beauty.

TUTTI: Your beauty! Why, you've only got to ask anyone which of us is the most beautiful and they're bound to say me.

FRUTTI: All right, ask someone. Ask him, down there in the bargain basement. (points to CONDUCTOR)

TUTTI: Very well. (to CONDUCTOR) Ooh-Ooh, I say - oh, he's rather handsome, isn't he? (fluttering eyelids at him) I say, Gorgeous, what's your name?

CONDUCTOR: My name? Charlie, (or whatever it is)

TUTTI: Well, Charlie, I'm sorry to bother you with such a silly question - I mean, I know you'll say me, but which of us is the most beautiful?

CONDUCTOR: Me.

TUTTI:	I've gone off him. What are you doing down there, anyway?
CONDUCTOR:	I'm looking after the music.
FRUTTI:	Music? Ah just what we wanted.
TUTTI:	What for?
FRUTTI:	So that we can sing a little song.
TUTTI:	Why?
FRUTTI:	No reason.
TUTTI:	Very well, a little song for no reason.

MUSIC 11. "SONG WITHOUT REASON"

(Music, "Pop Goes The Weasel", lyrics by John Crocker)

TUT & FRU:
We don't know why we're singing this song,
It has no rhyme or reason,
It's fairly short and rather long -
We like our toast with cheese on.

FRUTTI:
Airy-fairy, here I go,
Early in the morning,
Singing high and singing low -
Cabbages ain't worth pawning.

TUTTI:
Buns and beef are very nice,
Mix them well together,
Boil them on a cube of ice -
Ain't it lovely weather?

FRUTTI: Dance.

(They dance)

TUTTI: More dance.

(They dance again)

TUT & FRU: More song.
Now we come to the end of our song,
We hope you have enjoyed it,
Lest you think the moral wrong -
If you see a radish avoid it.

(They dance off into Inn. PRINCE and DANDINI enter U.R. having made a slight exchange of clothes. PRINCE carries a list)

PRINCE: Well, Dandini - I mean, your Highness, how does it feel to be a Prince?

DANDINI: Splendid, and as my first royal duty I shall just settle a little account with the - er - "landlord" here.

PRINCE: Why, how much do you owe?

DANDINI: I don't. She owes me - one kiss. (exit into Inn)

PRINCE: Well, I'd better start delivering the invitations. (consulting list) Who's first? The Baron Hardup of Hardup Hall and his daughters Tutti and Frutti. I wonder where Hardup Hall is? (looks off L) Perhaps this girl coming now will know. Why, what a lovely girl she is.

(PRINCE waits beside Inn as CINDERELLA enters L, carrying a large bundle of wood)

CINDERS: I think I've gathered almost too much. Still, I must hurry home with it or the kitchen fire will be out.

(PRINCE is about to speak when Fairy MUSIC 12 starts. He steps back behind Inn as FAIRY GODMOTHER enters D.R. disguised as an old woman, hobbling on a stick and carrying a few pieces of kindling wood)

FAIRY G: Alas, alack and dearie me,
Would my old eyes could better see;
The more I've sought the less I've found.

CINDERS: Good-day, good dame, you weary sound.
What is it that you wish to find?
Can I not help?

FAIRY G: Thy offer's kind.
'Tis just some kindling wood I seek,
But my poor eyes have grown so weak
That scarce three sticks I've gather'd yet.

CINDERS: Why then, how lucky we have met,
For see all this that I have here.
Please take it. (offers bundle)

FAIRY G: Oh, no, no, my dear.

CINDERS: Oh, please, I beg you, for my sake.

FAIRY G: To please thee then, thy wood I'll take.
(takes bundle)
For though my eyes are dim of sight
They yet can read thy heart aright,
And they see naught but goodness there.
Thy kindness worthy fruit shall bear,
And someday when thy hopes are low
I shall repay this debt I owe.

(FAIRY exits R. Music fades)

CINDERS: Poor old woman, I'm glad I was able to help her, but I wonder what she meant about repaying her debt when my hopes are low? Well, I mustn't stand dreaming here, I must gather some more wood.

(Crosses L and begins to gather wood. PRINCE comes out from behind Inn)

PRINCE: (bowing) Madam. (slight pause, bows again) Madam.

CINDERS: (turning) Oh, I'm sorry. Were you speaking to me?

PRINCE: Who else?

CINDERS: I didn't think it could be me. I've never been called "Madam" before. It does sound nice. I wonder, would you ... no - no, of course you wouldn't.

PRINCE: What wouldn't I?

CINDERS: Well, it's silly but - but - well, would you just say "Madam" to me again?

PRINCE: Certainly, (bowing) madam. I am - er - the Prince's valet, Dandini? May I ask who you are?

CINDERS: Cinderella.

PRINCE: Cinderella - what a delightful name. And where do you live, here in the wood?

CINDERS: No, I live at Hardup Hall. Baron Hardup is my father.

PRINCE: Why, here's a coincidence. I have to deliver invitations to Hardup Hall for the Royal Ball tomorrow night. My list mentions the Baron's two daughters, but neither is named Cinderella. How is that?

CINDERS: Oh, the invitations will be for my step-sisters. I should never be invited to a Royal Ball.

PRINCE: Then I shall see that you are invited to this one.

CINDERS: Oh no, please - they won't like it - I mean ...

PRINCE: No, I insist, and we shall dance together all night.

CINDERS: Oh yes, I should like that - very much. But now I must finish gathering my wood.

PRINCE: No, let me do it. (kneels beside her) I saw your kind action to that old lady and then I knew your heart was as lovely as your face.

MUSIC 13.   "I'M IN LOVE WITH A DREAM"

BOTH: I'm in love with a dream,
                        With a song, with a sigh,
                        And I laugh and I cry,
                        And I don't quite know why -
                   Wake me up! I'm in love with a dream.
                   I'm in love with a dream,
                        With the morn, with a star.
                        Oh it's near, yet so far -
                        I don't know where you are -
                   Wake me up! I'm in love with a dream.
                   Some lovely day from out of the blue,
                   My dream will enfold me, my dream will come true.
                        I'll open my eyes, and find with surprise -
                   I don't know who!
                   I'm in love with a dream.
                        O come quick! Can't you see
                        My dream has to be
                        Your reality?
                   Wake me up! I'm in love with a dream.

BOTH:	Suddenly the world is full of singing -
	   I don't know why.
	I seem to be waiting for someone to share
	All the happiness everywhere,
	   And I wait and I dream and I sigh -
	   But the world passes by.

	I'm in love with a dream, etc.

(At end of number TUTTI pokes her head through U.S. window in Inn, and FRUTTI through D.S. window)

TUTTI:	Oh! Look at that lovely man!
FRUTTI:	Ow! What a gorgeous brute!
TUT & FRU:	(jumping through windows and rushing at PRINCE) He's mine! (seeing CINDERELLA) Cinders!
TUTTI:	Cinders, what do you mean by lazing about here talking with a beautiful gent?
FRUTTI:	A magnificent hunk of male what you've got no right to talk to!
TUT & FRU:	Get home at once!
PRINCE:	I will come with you, if you like.
CINDERS:	I think perhaps you'd better not.

(Enter BUTTONS from Inn)

FRUTTI:	Certainly not. Buttons, you go off home with Cinderella.
BUTTONS:	All right. Let me take that wood for you, Cinders. (takes wood and almost collapses under weight) Well, for a bit of the way.

(He staggers off R after CINDERELLA)

TUTTI:	Fancy you thinking of going with her!
FRUTTI:	When you can stay here -
TUT & FRU:	With ME!
TUTTI:	(pulling PRINCE one way) Leave go! He's mine!
FRUTTI:	(pulling PRINCE other way) I saw him first!
TUTTI:	You didn't!)
FRUTTI:	I did!) (Tug o'war with PRINCE)
PRINCE:	Ladies! I fear I must leave you both. I have work to do.
FRUTTI:	Work? What work?
PRINCE:	I am the Prince's valet and -
FRUTTI:	Ah, royal work!

(Enter BARON from Inn)

Pa, this is the Prince's valet.

TUTTI: What is a valet, pa?

BARON: Oh, a sort of personal manservant.

TUT & FRU: A SERVANT? (both drop PRINCE's arm hurriedly)

FRUTTI: Tutti, we've been mixing with the lower orders.

TUTTI: Yes, I feel quite contimidated.

TUT & FRU: Come, sister. (they move away)

        (DANDINI enters from Inn with arm round MISS MUFFET)

DANDINI: Dear Landlord, sweet Landlord, I must leave for the
        hunt. Will you ask the stableman to bring round my horse?

MUFFET: Yes, but only if you promise not to ask her if she'd like
        to learn any secrets.

DANDINI: I promise.

        (MUFFET exits into Inn)

PRINCE: Er-hm- His Royal Highness, the Prince.

BARON: The Prince! Quickly, curtsey, girls.

        (TUTTI and FRUTTI curtsey. TUTTI goes extremely low and stays down)

        Three cheers for his Highness.

FRUTTI: (rising) Don't be stingy, make it four.

BARON: Any advance on four?

TUTTI: Five.

FRUTTI: Five and a half.

BARON: Five and a half I'm bid, who'll make it six? ... Nobody.
        Right. (absentmindedly knocking hunting crop on TUTTI's head) Going at
        five and a half. Going, going, gone! Hip-hip -

FRUTTI: Hooray, hooray, hooray, hooray, hooray, hoor.

DANDINI: My people, we thank you for your tremendous welcome.

BARON: Here, here!

DANDINI: And I - er - we can assure you that - er - that you can be
        assured that - er - that -

FRUTTI: There, there!

DANDINI: That we - I - we - all of us, appreciate it.

TUTTI: And very nicely put too.

DANDINI: (pointing to TUTTI) What is that down there?

FRUTTI: A sit down strike.

BARON: Oh, Tutti, do get up.

TUTTI: I can't. I got all mixed up going down.

(BARON and FRUTTI discover that her legs are entwined together and sort them out)

BARON: Your Highness, may I present my step-daughters, Tutti and Frutti?

PRINCE: (intercepting) Applications for introductions to the Prince must be made through me in triplicate.

BARON: Very well. Then may I, may I, may I?

PRINCE: May he, may he, may he?

DANDINI: He may, he may, he may.

BARON: Oh, goodie, goodie, goodie. Pom-tiddley-om-pom, pom-pom. I'm sorry.

(TUTTI and FRUTTI keep running round him as he introduces them)

Your Highness, this is Tutti, and this is Frutti, and this is Tutti, and this is Frutti, and this is Tutti and this is Frutti.

DANDINI: What a large family, Baron. Delighted to have met them all.

PRINCE: I must go and deliver these invitations. (bowing) Excuse me your Highness. I bid you good-day, ladies.

(TUTTI and FRUTTI sniff)

May I wish you a pleasant hunt?

(TUTTI and FRUTTI sniff harder)

Then I must wish you an unpleasant hunt. (bows and exits U. R.)

TUT & FRU: Eh?

DANDINI: Now we are assembled, let the hunt commence!

MUSIC 14. "A-HUNTING LET US GO"

(Traditional music, lyrics by John Crocker)

ALL: To horse, to horse! The hunt is up!
A-hunting let us go.

(MISS MUFFET enters from Inn with a stirrup cup. BARON crosses to her)

BARON: But ere we leave a stirrup cup
Would be a tasty thing to sup.

MUFFET: Oh yes, indeed, 'tis curds and whey.

BARON: In that case, not today.

ALL: Then a-hunting let us go!
With a yoicks and tallyho!

TUTTI: With yoicks?

FRUTTI: Yes, yoicks.

DANDINI: And tallyho!

ALL:	A-hunting let us go!
	Oh -
	We don't ken John Peel and don't give a toss
	Whether he's on or fallen off his hoss,
	But if we should fall, we hope it's on some moss,
	For the ground's very hard in the morning.
	So -
DANDINI:	Let's away on our chivey.
BARON:	Sing view-haloo, tantivy.

(Enter DOBBIN from above Inn)

TUTTI:	Oh, Dobbin -
FRUTTI:	Dobbin -
TUT & FRU:	Time to go -
ALL:	A-hunting, hunting, hunting, hunting, hunting,
	We will go!

(TUTTI and FRUTTI fight to get on DOBBIN, while they are doing so BARON gets on him instead and ALL exit U. R. as Hunt Ballet Music starts. In the ballet the leading dancer enters dressed as a Fox and is chased by the CHORUS, some as Hounds and some as Huntsmen in hobby-horse skirts and are joined by DANDINI, BARON, TUTTI and FRUTTI in similar skirts. The Ballet ends with the escape of the Fox)

ALL:	Oh, a hunting we did go,
	But the fox his heels did show,
	And horse and hounds were all too slow
	So a-drinking, drinking, drinking, drinking,
	Drinking, drinking, drinking now we'll go!

(As they dance off towards Inn -)

BLACKOUT

(Close traverse tabs. Fly in Scene Two frontcloth, if used)

Scene Two. A VILLAGE STREET

(Frontcloth or tabs. If cloth is used, tabs to begin)

(MUSIC 15. Enter BARON R, on DOBBIN)

BARON:　　　　　Whoa back, Dobbin.

(DOBBIN stops and BARON dismounts, very bandy)

Oh dear, my poor legs. I think I'd better take up the 'cello. I say, what a pretty dandelion. It'd do nicely for my buttonhole. I think I'll take it.

(AUDIENCE shout. DOBBIN shies, neighing loudly, kicks up a back leg which knocks over BARON and runs off L. BUTTONS runs on R. Open traverse tabs)

BUTTONS:　　　　Somebody at my dandelion again? Baron, you mustn't take that, it's mine. (helps BARON up) Still, it's lucky I caught you, this letter's just come for you. (hands BARON large letter)

BARON:　　　　　(opening it) Hm, I wonder who it's from? Good heavens! They're sending the Broker's Men. Buttons, I must nip and get some embrocation for my bot - my back. Wait here for me and keep an eye out for anybody looking like Broker's Men.

BUTTONS:　　　　Righto.

(BARON hobbles off R. BUTTONS puts a hand to his eyes and swings round to L scanning horizon)

Not a Broker's Man in sight.

(MUSIC 16. RAG, TAG AND BOBTAIL enter L)

RAG:　　　　　　Good-morning, we're the Broker's Men.

BUTTONS:　　　　(still very preoccupied with looking) Oh, yes.

RAG:　　　　　　Messrs Rag -

TAG:　　　　　　Tag -

BOBTAIL:　　　　And me.

RAG:　　　　　　And Bobtail, at your service. Our card. (puts card in BUTTONS' hand)

BUTTONS:　　　　Thank you.

RAG:　　　　　　We're trying to find Hardup Hall. I say it's that way.
　　(points to R)

TAG:　　　　　　And I say it's that way. (points L)

RAG:　　　　　　And he says - what do you say, Bobtail?

BOBTAIL:　　　　Oh - er - (nods vigorously) no.

RAG:　　　　　　What do you mean - oh - er - (nods) no?

BOBTAIL:　　　　Well - er - (shakes head vigorously) yes.

RAG:　　　　　　Hm, very helpful. (to BUTTONS) Perhaps you could tell us how to get to Hardup Hall?

BUTTONS: (still preoccupied, points off R.) Yes, first on the left that way.

RAG: (to TAG) There you are.

TAG: He's probably wrong. I wouldn't put it past 'em to move it.

RAG: Don't be silly. (confidentially to BUTTONS) You see, between you and me and the gatepost, we want to take them by surprise.

BOBTAIL: I say.

RAG: What?

BOBTAIL: I can't see a gatepost between you and him.

RAG: There isn't one.

TAG: Ah, I expect they've moved that too.

RAG: Nobody's moved anything. It's just an expression.

TAG: Then you should say, between you and me and the expression.

BOBTAIL: I've never seen a gatepost with an expression.

BUTTONS: (looking at card and suddenly realising) Hey, you're Broker's Men.

RAG: That's right. Messrs. Rag -

BUTTONS: Never mind that. You want to get to Hardup Hall, do you?

(BARON enters R.)

Well, how silly of me, of course Hardup Hall isn't that way (points R.) it's that way. (points L.)

BARON: What are you talking about? Hardup Hall is first on the left this way.

BUTTONS: Sh! Sh!

BARON: Well, I should know, I've lived there all my -

BUTTONS: (indicating the BARON is screwy) It's the second on the right down there and -

BARON: It's not! It's -

(BUTTONS claps a hand over BARON's mouth and whispers heavily in his ear)

Broker's Men! (to them) Ah, Hardup Hall, you said. Of course, that is second on the right down there -

BUTTONS: Then on to the traffic lights -

BARON: Turn left at the pillar-box -

BUTTONS: And there it is, dead opposite a railway sleeper.

BARON: You can't miss it.

(BARON and BUTTONS push BROKER's MEN off L.)

BAR & BUT: Phew!

BARON: Buttons, we must get home at once. Come, to horse, to horse!

BUTTONS: We haven't got any horses.

BARON: Then we must improvise. (leaps on BUTTONS' back) Giddyup there!

BUTTONS: OW! Mind where you're digging those spurs!

(He gallops off R. with BARON)

RAG: (off) Here we are, this is it.

(RAG, TAG and BOBTAIL enter at R. side of Auditorium and move down R. aisle towards front. HOUSELIGHTS UP)

Hardup Hall.

TAG: Are you sure?

RAG: Of course. (to Lady in AUDIENCE) Now then, madam, are you Baron Hardup? Oh, beg pardon, you wouldn't be, would you?

BOBTAIL: Ooh look, there's where we've just come from.

TAG: Ah, they've told us wrong. I knew they would.

(They climb up catwalk steps and MISS MUFFET enters L., studying a book. HOUSELIGHTS OUT.)

RAG: I say, miss.

MUFFET: Have we met before?

RAG: No.

MUFFET: Then I don't think we'd better. It isn't safe. The last time I met a man I hadn't met before he asked me to try kissing and I did and I liked it, so you see how dangerous it is.

RAG: But we only want to ask you if you know the way to Hardup Hall.

MUFFET: Oh. Well, I'm not very familiar with the district as yet, but I happen to have a street guide with me. (consults book) Let me see. Ah yes, you go straight along there. (points to R. aisle)

(HOUSELIGHTS UP. RAG, TAG and BOBTAIL descend catwalk and return up R. aisle in order BOBTAIL, TAG and RAG)

R, T & B: Straight along here.

MUFFET: And take the first to the right.

R, T & B: (turning along transverse aisle) First to the right.

MUFFET: I beg your pardon, second to the right.

R, T & B: Second to the right.

(RAG turns back and continues up R.aisle, while the others continue along transverse)

R, T & B: Here we are, second to the right.

(RAG exits at back of Auditorium. TAG and BOBTAIL turn right into L aisle at end of transverse aisle)

TAG: We've come to a dead end.

MUFFET: I'm so sorry, it can't be second to the right.

T & B: (turning back up L.aisle) Not second to the right.

MUFFET: It must be first to the right.

T & B: First to the right.

(TAG goes through exit at L.C. of Auditorium. BOBTAIL turns L, back into transverse aisle)

BOBTAIL: I've been this way before.

MUFFET: Oh dear, then perhaps it's not first to the right, after all.

BOBTAIL: Not first to the right.

MUFFET: It must be second to the right.

BOBTAIL: (turning right into R.aisle) Second to the right. Hey, where is everybody? Rag! Tag! Come back! Where are you? Come back! (runs up R aisle and exits at back of Auditorium)

MUFFET: Wait a minute. (turns book upside down) I should have been saying left all the time. (looks up) Oh, they've gone. What a pity, I wanted to ask them how to get back home. (exits L.)

R, T & B: (off) We're there!

(RAG enters at L.C. of Auditorium, TAG at R.back and BOBTAIL at L.back)

We're not. (they move towards catwalk)

RAG: This is ridiculous. We'll never get there at this rate.

TAG: I knew we wouldn't all along.

BOBTAIL: I think we should start from somewhere else.

RAG: But we don't seem to be able to get anywhere else.

TAG: What are we going to do then?

RAG: What can we do? Nothing.

(HOUSELIGHTS OUT when they are onstage again.)

TAG: Nothing?

RAG: Nothing.

BOBTAIL: Oh, goody, that's just what I like doing.

(Close traverse tabs slowly during number, fly out frontcloth)

MUSIC 17. "LET'S DO NOWT!"

R, T & B:
Let's do a lovely lot of nothing;
Let's do nothing really hard.
Let's make a ruling for the future
That expenditure of energy is barred.

RAG:
We've cakes of soap by Camay and we've tooth-
brushes by Tek,

TAG:
But in spite of toilet requisites we all appear a
wreck,

BOBTAIL:
'Cos we always feel much warmer with some dirt
around our neck -

R, T & B:
So let's do nowt!

Let's do a loverly lot of nothing;
Let's try to stand completely still.
Let's try to obviate excitement
Till our pulse-rate stands at something less
than nil.

RAG:
Some people crave for exercise and walk around
the town.

TAG:
I wouldn't do a silly thing like that for half-a-
crown!

BOBTAIL:
Why are we standing up? Let's sing the next verse
lying down -

R, T & B:
Yes, let's do nowt!

(They lie down)

Let's do a lovely lot of nothing.
Lots of nothing let us do.
Let's settle all our labour problems
And in future any kind of work eschew.

RAG:
For money we would simply like to wave a magic
wand,

TAG:
Till Ernie sent five thousand, since of money we
are fond.

BOBTAIL:
We'd be a bit surprised, because we've never
bought a Bond -

R, T & B:
But let's do nowt!

There's seventeen more verses, and each verse has
a refrain,
Then we ought to do a little dance, then from the
top again;
But singing silly songs like this is such an awful
strain -

So let's do nowt!

BLACKOUT

(Open traverse tabs)

Scene Three. THE KITCHEN AT HARDUP
HALL

(Fullset. Flat at C.back with opening in it concealed by a prop mangle, with a prop iron and a large bowl marked "EGGS" on top of it, containing prop eggs and one ping-pong ball. Prop ham hanging to R.of mangle, 2 saucepans hanging L.of it. Door flat R.of C.flat, and door flat L.of it, both doors opening onstage. Window wing R with casement window opening outwards. (For the transformation in Scene 7, this wing can be fitted on a swivel and swung round to show the reverse side painted as an exterior window). Fireplace L. (This can be a door flat minus the door and the opening covered with a black drape. In front of this is a truck on castors forming the hearth and on which are mounted side walls supporting a fire hood). 2 frying pans hang on L side of this fireplace, a besom broom leans against it and there is a prop poker on the hearth. 3 legged stool in front of fireplace. Table C, with prop fish and prop rolling pin on it.

(MUSIC 18. CINDERELLA discovered on stool putting some sticks on fire)

CINDERS: There, that's saved the fire. Now I suppose I'd better start the cleaning.

(She picks up the broom and begins to sweep. EFFECT 1. Knock at door U.R.)

I do hope this isn't one of father's creditors. (opens U.R. door a crack) I'm sorry, the Baron isn't here, but I'm sure he'll pay you as soon as he can. (shuts door)

PRINCE: (pushing door open a little) But I -

CINDERS: It's no use waiting, I'm afraid. The Baron said he wouldn't be back for hours, perhaps days, weeks even. (pushes door to)

PRINCE: (pushing door open again) But I haven't come to see the Baron. I've come to see you.

CINDERS: (opening door fully) Oh, I'm so sorry, I didn't realise. Please come in.

PRINCE: (entering) Thank you.

CINDERS: (shuts door) Would you like to sit down? There's only this little stool. It's wobbly in one leg, but the other two are quite sound.

PRINCE: Oh - er - thank you. (sits gingerly on stool) I've brought the invitations for the ball.

CINDERS: Oh, how wonderful! Oh, dear.

PRINCE: What's the matter?

CINDERS: I've just thought. All the ladies will have lovely dresses and I haven't got many clothes. In fact, these are all -

PRINCE: Whatever you wear you will look beautiful, Cinderella. And for myself, I should always like to remember you just as you are now.

MUSIC 19 "I WILL ALWAYS REMEMBER"

PRINCE &
CINDERS:
I will always remember the way you look today.
I'll remember this moment for ever come what may.
The strange and lovely feeling that held me from the
start,
The words that were a message to my heart.
I will always remember the laughter in your eyes,
And the things that they told me of Paradise.
Of all the things in my life I may or may not do,
I will always remember the day when I met you.

(TUTTI and FRUTTI enter U.L.)

TUTTI: Now then, what's all this gaiety?

FRUTTI: Who's this you're larking around with?

PRINCE: (bowing) Your humble servant, ladies.

TUTTI: Oh, it's that low servant fellow.

FRUTTI: That common valet.

CINDERS: He's not low or common.

FRUTTI: That's enough from you, my girl. Followers in the kitchen, indeed!

PRINCE: Ladies, I've called to deliver your invitations to the Ball at the Palace tomorrow night.

FRUTTI: What, the palace? A royal ball!

PRINCE: (putting invitation cards on table) Yes, one for Miss Tutti, one for Miss Frutti and one for Cinderella.

TUTTI: One for Cinders?

PRINCE: Yes, every lady in the land is invited.

TUTTI: Every lady, yes.

PRINCE: (looking TUTTI and FRUTTI in the eye) Well, sometimes it's a little difficult to say just who is a lady, isn't it? (smiles and bows to them) Good-day, ladies. (kissing CINDERELLA's hand) Goodbye, Cinderella. I shall look forward to seeing you at the ball. (exits U.R.)

FRUTTI: I think he's a bit cheeky, you know.

TUTTI: Never mind him. We'll never be ready in time. I've hardly a rag fit to wear.

FRUTTI: Nor me. Cinders, you must reorganise my orange organdie.

TUTTI: And titivate my tartan taffeta.

CINDERS: Very well, Tutti. And, Tutti, could - could you lend me one of your old dresses, one of your very old ones?

TUTTI: Certainly not. What do you want it for?

CINDERS: To go to the ball in.

FRUTTI: But you're not going to the ball.

CINDERS: Why not?

TUTTI: Because you haven't anything to wear.

FRUTTI: (taking up card and tearing it into little pieces) And because you haven't an invitation card.

CINDERS: Frutti, please!

FRUTTI: Now sweep up all those little bits of paper.

CINDERS: I - I - oh. (fighting back tears, runs off U. L.)

TUTTI: Now what's the matter with the girl?

(BARON runs on U. R.)

BARON: Buttons! Tutti! Frutti! Everybody! They're here!

TUTTI: Who's here?

BARON: Where's Buttons? I sent him ahead to tell you. We shall be besieged at any minute!

TUTTI: Oh, good! Who by?

BARON: The Brokers Men!

FRUTTI: (looking out of window) Ooh! There's someone coming now.

BARON: (siezing rolling-pin) It's them! Stand by to repel all boarders!

FRUTTI: Oh, are we taking in lodgers? (gets down prop ham from U. R.)

TUTTI: (taking prop fish from table) I've always wanted to give someone a slap in the belly with a wet fish.

BARON: Stand by!

(They get in position by door U. R. Door is pushed open)

BARON: Now!)
BUTTONS: (entering) Hello - help!) (together)
)

(BUTTONS turns and runs off, the others leap forward to strike. TUTTI hits BARON: BARON hits FRUTTI: FRUTTI hits TUTTI. All fall dropping their improvised weapons and sit rubbing their heads. BUTTONS peers cautiously through window)

BUTTONS: Anything the matter?

BARON: Buttons, where have you been? Come in at once and fasten that window.

(BUTTONS enters and fastens window. Others rise)

The rest of you, barricade the doors, putty-up the keyholes, flood the moat, raise the drawbridge and lower the portcullis!

BUTTONS: But we haven't got a moat.

TUTTI: Or a drawbridge.

FRUTTI: Or a port-what-you-said.

BARON: I don't care - do it! Block up that door!

(TUTTI, FRUTTI and BUTTONS run C table in front of U.L. door)

And that one!

(They run table in front of U.R. door)

I thought I told you to block that one?

(They run table back to U.L. door)

But what about this one?

(They break table in middle, leave half in front of U.L. door and block U.R. door with other half)

Now, defend all the doors and windows!

(BUTTONS picks up rolling-pin and takes up a position by window. TUTTI goes to defend U.L. door with her fish, FRUTTI remains by U.R. door with ham. BARON stands by fireplace holding up poker. **EFFECT 2.** A loud knocking is heard off R)

BUTTONS: It's them!

BARON: Well, we're ready for 'em. Just let 'em try and get in, that's all, just let 'em try!

(RAG and TAG enter down chimney, knocking over BARON. Knocking off R continues)

BARON, T & F, and BUTTONS: Bamboozled!

RAG: (shouting to R) You can stop knocking now, Bobtail, we're in.

(Knocking stops as BOBTAIL enters down chimney behind them)

BOBTAIL: Beg pardon?

TAG: (shouting to R) He said you can stop knocking.

BOBTAIL: (shouting in their ears) I have.

RAG & TAG: (they jump and turn and wiggle their fingers in their ears) Don't do that.

BOBTAIL: Sorry. (sits rather forlornly on stool)

RAG: (politely raising hat) Good morning. We've come to take the furniture.

TAG: And I hope it's not too heavy.

(RAG takes half table from door U.R. TAG the half from door U.L.)

RAG & TAG: Excuse us.

TUT & FRU: Not at all.

(RAG and TAG exit U. R. with table halves)

BARON: Well, don't just stand there being polite - get the furniture back! (shoves poker in fire)

(TUTTI throws fish down to fireplace, FRUTTI drops ham U. R. and they exit through U. R. door. BUTTONS puts down rolling-pin and opens window, where BARON crosses to join him. RAG and TAG return U. R. and go to stool)

RAG: This next.

RAG & TAG: Heave together - hup!

(They exit U. R. carrying stool with BOBTAIL on it. TUTTI and FRUTTI substitute table made in one piece, through window to BARON and BUTTONS)

TUT & FRU: Here you are.

BAR & BUT: Thank you kindly.

ALL 4:   Shove it in - over.

(BARON and BUTTONS replace table C, and return to window. RAG and TAG enter U. R. and go to table)

RAG: To you.

TAG: From me.

RAG & TAG: Heave together - hup!

(RAG and TAG exit U. R. with table. TUTTI and FRUTTI push stool through to BARON and BUTTONS)

TUTTI: To you.

FRUTTI: From us.

TUT & FRU: With love.

ALL 4:   Shove it in - over!

(As BARON and BUTTONS take stool BOBTAIL climbs over window-sill)

BOBTAIL: (raising hat to TUTTI and FRUTTI) Excuse me.

TUT & FRU: (inclining heads politely) With pleasure.

(BOBTAIL sits on stool and BARON and BUTTONS carry him to fireplace on it. RAG and TAG enter U. R. and go to stool, as BARON and BUTTONS go back)

RAG: This next.

TAG: Too many tables and stools for my liking.

RAG & TAG: Heave together - hup!

(They exit carrying stool with BOBTAIL on it. TUTTI and FRUTTI start to push table through to BARON and BUTTONS)

TUT & FRU: And again.

    (RAG and TAG return unexpectedly from U.R.)

BAR & BUT,
TUT & FRU: Rumbled!

BAR & BUT: Shove it back - over!

    (BARON and BUTTONS push table back and go through window after it)

RAG: After 'em!

TAG: We'll only fall and break our necks!

RAG: Never mind!

    (They follow through window. TUTTI and FRUTTI enter U.R. carrying stool with BOBTAIL on it, which they replace by fire and BARON and BUTTONS run on and replace table in C)

BARON: Quick, the door!

    (Runs to R.door and BUTTONS to L.door so that they collide above table, fall over and quickly jump up again)

Not that one, this one!

    (Both run to shut R.door just as TAG is about to enter. He staggers back with a cry)

Just in time!

    (RAG bursts in through U.L. door)

RAG: Not quite.

TAG: (jumping in through window, holding nose) You hit my nose.

BARON: Out with 'em! (picks up ham from U.R)

    (BARON and BUTTONS run to grab TAG, who jumps out of window again, shutting it in their faces so that they fall back. BUTTONS picks up rolling-pin. At the same time, TUTTI picks up fish and hits RAG with it, who staggers back. She turns to FRUTTI who congratulates her)

TUTTI: First blood to us!

    (While her back is turned RAG plucks poker from fire, which has had a red end put on it, and touches TUTTI on bottom with it. She drops fish and clutches her bottom)

OW!

    (RAG chases her clockwise round table with poker. FRUTTI grabs broom and follows on hitting RAG with it. BARON has moved up and is now in front of U.R. door as TAG flings it open, knocks him over and rushes in)

BUTTONS: (moving up, waving rolling-pin) Hey!

    (MUSIC 20. TAG plucks rolling-pin from his hand and follows on behind FRUTTI hitting her with it. BUTTONS moves to mangle, seizes prop iron and follows TAG hitting him with that. ALL chase twice round table

with shouts and cries. During chase, BARON rises and tries to
assist by hitting somebody with ham, but the first time uses such a
forcible preparatory back-swing that the ham flies from his hand, and
the second time hits BUTTONS by mistake and he staggers away.
At this moment BOBTAIL inadvertently puts his foot out and trips
RAG, who falls dropping the poker.
FRUTTI vaults over RAG using broom as a pole vault and then
flinging it aside.
TAG falls over RAG losing rolling-pin.
TUTTI and FRUTTI continue round table and grab a saucepan each
from U. L. and TUTTI takes ping-pong ball from egg bowl on mangle.
They stop when they are L of table.
As soon as they have scrambled up RAG and TAG take the frying pans
from the fireplace and chase after TUTTI and FRUTTI until they are on
R side of table. Music stops)

TUTTI: Service!

(She serves ball and the four play a doubles match with their saucepans
and frying-pans. BARON has been helping BUTTONS to recover and
now with the ham and the iron they knock down RAG and TAG)

TUT & FRU: Game, set and match to us!

BARON: Through the mangle with 'em!

(All four pick up RAG)

TUT & FRU: By the legs -

BAR & BUT: By the arms -

ALL 4: Heave together - hup!

(They carry RAG to mangle)

BAR & BUT: Hold him steady!

TUT & FRU: Turn!

(BUTTONS turns mangle, TUTTI and FRUTTI push RAG through and pull
back flat effigy, which they carry to door while BARON and BUTTONS
drag TAG to mangle)

(swinging effigy) Swing together - hout!

BUTTONS: Hold him steady!

BARON: Turn!

(BUTTONS turns mangle, BARON pushes TAG through. Both pull back
2nd effigy and throw it to TUTTI and FRUTTI)

BAR & BUT: To you.

TUT & FRU: Thank you. Swing together - hout!

(They throw 2nd effigy out of U.R. door)

ALL 4: VICTORY!

(They turn and see BOBTAIL sitting on stool.)

ALL 4:   Oh.

BOBTAIL: You are mean. You haven't done me.

(Huffily he crosses up to mangle and pushes himself through)

BLACKOUT

(MUSIC 21. Close traverse tabs)

Scene Four. OUTSIDE HARDUP HALL

(Frontcloth (tabs to open) or tabs. There is a notice - "FLUNKEYS WANTED - APPLY PALACE", C of cloth, (or on board set during blackout if tabs are used) MUSIC 22)

(Enter RAG and TAG R, rather the worse for wear)

RAG: I don't think we came off too well there.

TAG: No, I knew we'd make a muck of it.

RAG: Well, we was overpowered by superior numbers.

TAG: I was overpowered by being put through a mangle.

RAG: Here, where's Bobtail?

TAG: Isn't he here? Coo, I bet the mangle did for him. (Reverently removes hat) Poor old Bobtail.

RAG: (does likewise) Poor old Bobtail.

(They both wipe away a tear as BOBTAIL enters R, very perkily and moves behind to between them. Open traverse tabs)

BOBTAIL: Hullo.

RAG & TAG: (not looking up, still weeping) Hullo, Bobtail.

BOBTAIL: Can we go through the mangle again?

TAG: Ah, Bobtail, your mangling days are over.

RAG: Yes - yes, you've been through your last mangle.

BOBTAIL: (disappointed) Why?

RAG & TAG: (almost too overcome) Because you're - you're ... (suddenly realising and looking up, indignantly) You're alive! (hitting him with their hats) How dare you!

BOBTAIL: I only wanted to go through the mangle again. I liked it. It tickled.

RAG: Tickled!

TAG: It didn't tickle me.

RAG: Anyway, we haven't time to go playing about with mangles now. After that last shambles we must look for a new job. (sees notice and points) Here, that'll do us. They want some flunkeys at the Palace.

TAG: Flunkeys? I couldn't be a flunkey. I'm the worse flunkey what ever flunked.

RAG: Nonsense you're just flunking it. We'll go to the Palace right away. Come on.

(He moves L, TAG follows him)

Wait a minute, I've just seen a dandelion. I think I'll pick it.

(RAG and TAG turn back as he crosses to it. AUDIENCE shout.)

(BUTTONS runs on L.)

BUTTONS: Somebody at my dandelion again? Ah, I'll soon scare them off. (he runs off L.)

BOBTAIL: I say, it's a very noisy dandelion, isn't it? Did you hear it shouting just then?

(BUTTONS returns L., disguised as a ghost with a sheet over his head)

BUTTONS: Whoo! Whoo!

(RAG turns and sees him)

RAG: Aaah! Help!

(He turns and runs off R., in front of TAG)

TAG: What's the matter with him?

BUTTONS: (moving beside TAG) Whoo! Whoo!

TAG: (turns and sees him) Aaah! Help! (runs off R.)

BUTTONS: (moving beside BOBTAIL) Whoo! Whoo!

BOBTAIL: Brr! Nasty wind getting up.

(BUTTONS taps him on shoulder. He turns)

Hullo.

BUTTONS: (waggling sheeted arms menacingly) Whoo!

BOBTAIL: Pardon?

BUTTONS: WHOOO!

BOBTAIL: What?

BUTTONS: (takes off sheet in disgust) WHOOOO!

BOBTAIL: Aaah! Help! (runs off R.)

BUTTONS: Well, that's got rid of them - at last. (throws sheet off-stage) It's very nice of you to look after my dandelion so well. I think I'll just give it a little fertiliser while I'm here.

(Brings on a large packet marked "FERTILISER" and puts the packet in the pot. Music whizz. The dandelion shoots up as high as possible)

BUTTONS: Ooh! Very strong fertiliser.

(Removes packet from pot and the dandelion descends)

That's better.

(Puts fertiliser packet off R.)

Very leafy, isn't it? I wonder if some of the animals in my zoo would eat the leaves. You haven't seen my zoo, have you? This is it.

(Brings on a large box with a sign on top - "BUTTONS ZOO". It is divided into four small cages marked - "LIZARDS", "MICE", "RAT" and "EMPTY".)

BUTTONS: This is the reptile house here with two green lizards. Then we come to the rodent terrace with two white mice here and one grey rat there which brings us next to the - er - the empty. Very rare they are. Of course, it's not a very big zoo yet, but never mind, they're very intelligent animals. In fact, I'm even teaching them to sing. Yes, like this -

(Close traverse tabs slowly during number. Fly out cloth)

<u>MUSIC 23</u>. "SING"

Fill your tank and sing, "Hip-hip-hoo-
-Ray doh te soh fah me ray doh",
You will thank me for the tip
And say that it's the way that it's to go.
If your vocal chords proper are
You can use them in opera.
I do my scales each morning
And I'll entertain you for a modest fee,
Though I am very certain you can do it just as
well as me.

<u>BLACKOUT</u>

(Open traverse tabs)

Scene Five. THE UGLY SISTERS BOUDOIR

(Half-set. (This could be inset in kitchen) cloth or flats at back. Wing L. and wing R. Dressing table L.C, on which is a prop table-mirror, a hand-mirror, a hairbrush, a mop-head powder puff, some prop cosmetic pots and a coathanger. Set underneath it is a large tin marked "BICARBONATE OF SODA", a bottle of Guinness, a frying-pan and pancake, some brown paper, a toy pistol and a cannon. Dressing table R.C. on which is a prop table-mirror, a hand mirror, a mop-head powder puff and some prop cosmetic pots. Set underneath it is a large tin marked "GUNPOWDER", a Flit syringe, a roll-on and a toy machine gun)

(TUTTI at L table and FRUTTI at R, both in dressing gowns, are discovered making-up)

FRUTTI: You know, Tutti, I think I ought to have given my face a mud-pack.

TUTTI: I thought you had. I'm trying a pancake make-up. (produces the frying-pan, flips up the pancake and slaps it onto her face) How does it look?

FRUTTI: Much better. It hides your entire face. I've had some new powder given me. I was told it was just what I needed. (brings out a large tin marked "GUNPOWDER")

TUTTI: Yes, dear, I'm sure it is, but I think I prefer mine.

FRUTTI: Is it good?

TUTTI: Very. If it comes off it repeats itself.

(Produces the "BICARB" tin and they start powdering with their mop-heads, raising large clouds of powder)

Now just a touch of perfume. (brings up the Guinness bottle; dabs some behind her ears, on her wrists, pours some down her bosom and takes a swig)

FRUTTI: I prefer my scent spray. (brings up the Flit syringe and sprays herself liberally with it including down her throat) And now we're ready to get dressed.

(They rise and take off their dressing-gowns, which they throw off L & R, displaying ludicrous underwear)

TUTTI: Tighten my corset for me, dear.

(FRUTTI gives a good hard tug at the strings and pulls TUTTI over)

Careful Frutti.

FRUTTI: Well, hold on to something, then.

(TUTTI holds on to L. side of pros arch and FRUTTI pulls with her foot in TUTTI's back. TUTTI makes faces of excruciating agony)

Can you still breathe?

TUTTI: Yes.

FRUTTI: Not tight enough. (pulls harder) Can you breathe now?

TUTTI: No!

FRUTTI: That's all right then, I'll tie off.

(She pounces on TUTTI knocking her over and ties the strings)

There we are. Now I'll get my roll-on on.

(She gets it from dressing-table and bends to step into it, then suddenly clutches her back in pain. TUTTI rises)

Ow! Help! My lumbago's caught me bending! Help!

TUTTI: How awkward. Does it hurt?

FRUTTI: Yes, it's painful in the extreme.

TUTTI: So I see. Well of course, the best thing for lumbago is to iron it over brown paper. (calling off L) Buttons, bring a hot iron here.

BUTTONS: (off L) Righto.

TUTTI: (rummaging behind her dressing table) I think there's some brown paper here.

FRUTTI: It would happen the night we have to go to the ball. I can't dance like this.

TUTTI: How do you know? You haven't tried yet. (finds paper)

(BUTTONS runs on L, with prop iron)

BUTTONS: Here you are.

TUTTI: Ah, now we'll soon have you right again. (irons FRUTTI over paper) How's that, dear?

FRUTTI: Oh, it's much better already. Could you do it a little higher up now?

TUTTI: What did you say, dear? (leans forward, letting the paper fall and resting the iron on FRUTTI's behind)

FRUTTI: I said, just a little higher up.

TUTTI: Oh, I see, it's spread, has it?

FRUTTI: Yes, I want it now in about the middle of my - OOOOOOOWWWWWWW! Help! Help! I'm on fire! There's embers in my enders!

(BUTTONS runs off L. TUTTI seizes the iron from FRUTTI and reveals a large black scorch mark)

TUTTI: Oh, what a pity it's ruined your petty.

FRUTTI: It's ruined something else that's not so petty! Somebody do something, quick!

BUTTONS: (off L) It's all right, leave it to me!

(A bell clangs off L, and BUTTONS scoots on on the scooter, ringing a bell and wearing a fireman's helmet. The scooter carries a stirrup pump and a bucket. He starts to pump water onto FRUTTI)

FRUTTI: AAAHHH! Are you trying to drown me?

TUTTI: That'll do, Buttons.

BUTTONS: Righto. (scoots off L)

TUTTI: Better now, dear?

FRUTTI: Oh yes, I feel fine. I've been burnt to a cinder, drenched to the skin, caught pneumonia and still can't move - but, of course, I never felt better in my life.

TUTTI: Ah well, perhaps if I administer a slight shock -

(Kicks FRUTTI who jumps up clutching herself)

FRUTTI: Ow! I think you've dislocated something vital.

TUTTI: Never mind, it's got you going again.

FRUTTI: I've still got to get this wretched roll-on on.

TUTTI: Let me help you, then.

(She helps FRUTTI into roll-on, in the process getting one of her own legs in it and, extricating that, one of her arms gets caught, until finally the roll-on is on properly)

TUTTI: What a palaver! We'll never get to the ball tonight, at this rate. We'd better get Cinders to help us into our dresses.

FRUTTI: Yes, mine first.

TUTTI: No, mine. I'm the eldest.

FRUTTI: That's easy to see.

TUTTI: Don't you insult me like that. (slaps FRUTTI)

FRUTTI: And don't you slap me. (slaps TUTTI)

TUTTI: Well, don't you slap me, then. (slaps FRUTTI)

(Their slapping develops into boxing as BUTTONS enters L)

BUTTONS: Girls! Girls!

(They take no notice and continue fighting. BUTTONS picks up hairbrush from L dressing-table and uses it as a microphone)

And here we are for the big fight. On my left - the Terrible Tutti. On my right - the Frightful Frutti. Terrible Tutti leads with a left to the bodice, but Frightful Frutti blocks it with a right to the corset bones. Now they're getting in a huddle; now they're in a huddle; now they're out of the huddle and just in a muddle. This is terrific! Terrible Tutti's going in to attack again. She lands a left and a right and a right and a left and a foot. This is sheer murder! But Frightful Frutti's rallying, she hits back and now she hits front. I've never seen anything quite like this before. They're closing in again

BUTTONS: (continued) - quite close now - very close - too close -
OW!

(TUTTI and FRUTTI hit BUTTONS and he staggers off L. They each
pick up the coathangers from their dressing tables)

FRUTTI: Have at you!

(They commence duelling. TUTTI gets past FRUTTI's guard)

TUTTI: Touché!

(FRUTTI sprays TUTTI with the Flit syringe)

FRUTTI: Douché!

(TUTTI starts throwing cosmetic pots at FRUTTI. FRUTTI retaliates
with hers, lobbing them like hand grenades. Both get down behind
their dressing-tables. TUTTI brings up a toy pistol and starts banging
away with it. FRUTTI brings up her machine-gun. BUTTONS runs on
L, wearing a tin-hat and carrying a bugle)

BUTTONS: Call out the reserves! (blows a call on the bugle) Ugh!
They got me! (Clutches his breast and falls dramatically)

(TUTTI produces her prop cannon. EFFECT 3. Loud explosion.
BLACKOUT. LIGHTS UP. Various objects fall from the flies.
BUTTONS is holding up a white flag. TUTTI & FRUTTI, with blackened
faces, sit with their dressing-table mirrors crashed around their
necks. Enter BARON L)

BARON: All spick and span for the ball, my loves?

BLACKOUT

(MUSIC 24. Close traverse tabs. Fly in Scene Six frontcloth, if used)

Scene Six. THE SERVANTS' HALL AT THE PALACE

(Frontcloth or tabs. If cloth is used open tab as soon as convenient during scene)

(Enter PRINCE L. with a list and a pencil)

PRINCE: Well, either Dandini works harder than I thought or he wants to make sure I do. What's next? (consults list) Clean the royal boots. Done that. (ticks list) Iron the royal shirt. Scorched that. (ticks) Press the royal trousers. Tore those. (ticks) Ah, here we are. Interview new maids and prospective flunkeys.

(MUSIC 25. Enter RAG, TAG and BOBTAIL R.)

Hullo, are you prospective flunkeys?

RAG: That's right.

PRINCE: Then perhaps you could give me a demonstration of your flunkeying. Opening doors for instance. Can you open doors?

RAG: Opening doors? Our speciality. I'll show you. (indicating C) There's a door here, right?

PRINCE: Right.

RAG: I grasps the handle thus, right? (mimes it)

PRINCE: Right.

RAG: And I gives the handle a little rattle, thus -

(Mimes rattling handle. EFFECT 4. Rattle off)

And then - (stops, realises and looks down at hand) A little rattle, thus -

(Mimes it again. EFFECT 5. Rattle off)

Hm. Amazingly vivid imagination I have. Well, then I turns the handle -

(As he mimes this, EFFECT 6. Squeaky handle off)

'Strordinary. And I flings it open.

(Mimes this. Music whizz and drum crash. TAG falls as if struck by the door)

TAG: Now look what you've done. (rises) You want to see if there's anybody on the other side before you start flinging open doors.

RAG: How can I see if there's anybody on the other side if I don't open it first?

TAG: Well, you could walk round and take a look, couldn't you?

RAG: Don't be daft. If you think it's so easy, you just show us how you'd open a door.

TAG: All right. I grasps the handle thus, and then - and then -

(Strains to open door, rattling handle. EFFECT 7. Rattle off)

It won't open. (bends and peers through "keyhole") It's locked.

RAG: Then unlock it.

TAG: (peering) I can't. The key's on the other side.

RAG: Well, walk round and get it.

TAG: Don't be a darn fool, what do you think there's a door here for if you can just walk round it?

RAG: Aah! (rolling up sleeves) I'll pulverate you!

(Rushes at TAG and falls back as if he has run into a door. Drum crash) Ouch!

TAG: (walking round and helping him up) I told you, it's locked.

RAG: How did you get here then?

TAG: I walked round, of course.

RAG: (covering face with hands) It's not fair! It's not fair!

PRINCE: There, there. Perhaps we'd better try something else. How about announcing? Can you do that?

RAG: Announcing? Our extra speciality. Bobtail, show the - Bobtail! Wake up!

(BOBTAIL has fallen asleep leaning against pros arch R, and now wakes hurriedly and crosses to C.)

BOBTAIL: Eh? What? Yes. No. Oh. Hullo.

RAG: Bobtail, show the gent some announcing.

PRINCE: Suppose I were the Prince. How would you announce me?

BOBTAIL: I don't know. I don't know what announce means.

RAG: Announce just means say in a loud voice.

BOBTAIL: Oh, just say in a loud voice.

PRINCE: That's it. Now announce me.

BOBTAIL: ME!

RAG: Well, go on.

BOBTAIL: I've gone on.

RAG: I mean, announce him.

BOBTAIL: HIM!

RAG: What are you playing at?

BOBTAIL: I'm not playing at anything. You said announce meant say in a loud voice and he said announce "Me", so I did, and you said announce "Him", so I did and now you turn nasty. I was only doing my best. (dissolves into tears)

TAG: (comforting BOBTAIL. To RAG) There now, you've upset him. What d'you want to do that for?

RAG: (turning on PRINCE) Yes, what d'you want to do that for?

PRINCE: But I -

RAG: Poor old Bobtail.

(He walks into door. Drum crash)

Ow! Oh, of course, it's locked on this side.

(Mimes turning key in lock. **EFFECT 8. Lock turning off.** RAG walks through to comfort BOBTAIL)

It's all right, Bobtail. We won't take the rotten old job. Not for a hundred pounds a week each, we won't.

PRINCE: Well, actually the job only pays ne pound a week each.

R, T & B: One? Done.

RAG: We'll start right away. Come on, lads, we're in the money.

(They exit R. RAG returns)

RAG: So sorry. Left the door open.

(Shuts it. **EFFECT 9. Door slam off.** RAG exits R)

PRINCE: I can't see a door there.

(DANDINI enters R)

Ah, Dandini. Can you see a -

(DANDINI walks into "door". Drum crash)

DANDINI: (rubbing nose) Ow!

PRINCE: Um. I'd better leave it open for safety.

(Opens door. **EFFECT 10. Squeaky hinge off**)

DANDINI: I came to see how you were getting on.

PRINCE: Well, I've just done the flunkeys, now I'm waiting to interview the new maids.

(Enter MISS MUFFET L)

Ah, are you a new maid?

MUFFET: Well, I'm certainly not an old one, if that's what you're implying. I'm looking for the royal valet, Dandini. At least, I think I am.

PRINCE: How delightful, that's me.

MUFFET: Oh dear, then I'm not looking for you. I'm looking for the Prince.

DANDINI: (crossing PRINCE to her) How even more delightful, that's <u>me.</u> You may leave us, Dandini.

PRINCE: But, your Highness, what about the new maids?

DANDINI: (taking list from PRINCE) I'll interview them for you. Off you go, Dandini.

(He pushes PRINCE off R)

MUFFET: Are you quite, quite sure he's Dandini?

DANDINI: Oh, absolutely.

MUFFET: How very provoking. You see, I rather liked you. But I'm only an innkeeper and innkeepers and Princes can't like each other.

DANDINI: Can't they? What are we to do then?

MUFFET: I don't know. Start hating each other, I suppose.

DANDINI: I've a better idea. I'll promote you. Kneel down a moment.

(Mystified, she does so. He touches her on shoulder with the list rolled-up)

Arise, Lady Muffet.

(She rises)

How's that?

MUFFET: I don't know. Should I feel different? I've never been a lady before.

DANDINI: (laughs) You can get used to it at the ball tonight. But do be careful at the ball not to fall in love with the Prince, won't you?

MUFFET: But I've fallen in love with you already.

DANDINI: Splendid, but I may be deposed before tonight.

MUFFET: What?

DANDINI: Well, you can't always be sure of things, can you? There's one thing I am sure of, though - that you're the girl for me.

MUFFET: That's a pity. I'm not at all sure you're the boy for me.

(Close traverse tabs slowly during number. Fly out front cloth)

MUSIC 26. "LOVE LETTERS"

DANDINI: There was Jane and there was Penny,
There was Pam and Jill and Jenny,
    There were girls with ev'ry sort of name right
                through the alphabet;
There was Paula, there was Heather -
Fifty-seven altogether -
    But of all the girls I've ever known you're just
                the finest yet!

A B C D E F G -
I think that you're the very girl for me.
I only hope and pray you will agree,
    For that would be divine.

DANDINI: (continued)
U V W X Y Z -
The very thought of you goes to my head.
I'll never be content till we are wed
And I can call you mine.

MUFFET: A B C D E F G -
I'm not at all convinced you're right for me
We'll have to wait a little while and see
Before our lives entwine
U V W X Y Z -
I rather think my face is going red!
I seem to like the final words you said
About your being mine.

I have been around for ages,
And there's several hundred pages
    In the catalogue of all the many fellows I have
                                        known.
Some were slow and some were active,
Some were plain and some attractive,
    But I've never met a fellow yet to call my own.

Jack was quaint and Tim was charming,
Bill was thoroughly alarming,
    And old Peter wasn't bad except his nose was on
                                        the side.
Dennis thing was too emphatic,
Geoff had spiders in his attic,
    And to not a single one of them would I be bride.
There was Gerry, there was Larry,
There was Tom and Dick and Harry;
    There were some I met by accident and some were
                                        by design;
But of all the whole collection
I'm inclin'd in your direction,
    And it wouldn't be a bad idea to call you mine!

BLACKOUT

(Open traverse tabs)

Scene Seven. THE KITCHEN AT HARDUP
HALL

(As before, but with a wood wing set out of sight behind fireplace and cut-out ground-row of garden background along back of rostrum. BUTTONS' zoo is set above the fireplace and a large pumpkin hangs above it. There is a ragged cloth on the one piece table C, also a newspaper, a cup of tea, a bowler hat, a pair of shoes and a tin of boot polish and a brush)

(BUTTONS discovered at the table polishing the shoes)

BUTTONS:　　　　Boots, huh! I'm not a boots, I'm a buttons. (puts shoe down) Now for his hat. (picks up bowler and starts putting polish onto it) Difficult to get a good shine on this, though. Well, that'll have to do. (puts hat down) Whew! I've been on the go all evening. (lifts cup) I poured this cup of tea half an hour ago and I haven't touched it yet. (puts cup to lips)

BARON:　　　　　(off D.L.) Buttons!

BUTTONS:　　　　(puts down cup) Here we go again. Coming! (runs off D.L.)

TUT & FRU:　　　(off U.L.) Buttons!

BUTTONS:　　　　(off D.L.) Coming! (runs on and exits U.L. above fireplace)

BARON:　　　　　(off) Buttons!

BUTTONS:　　　　(off U.L.) Coming! (runs on and exits D.L.)

TUT & FRU:　　　(off) Buttons!

BUTTONS:　　　　(off D.L.) Coming! (runs on) If only I had a deed poll handy I'd change my name.

TUT & FRU:　　　(off) BUTTONS!

BUTTONS:　　　　All right, coming! (runs off U.L.)

(MUSIC 27. DOBBIN cautiously pushes his head round above window U.R. BUTTONS returns from U.L. and DOBBIN hastily withdraws head)

(stops) What am I doing? He hasn't called yet. (starts to run off U.L.)

BARON:　　　　　(off) Buttons!

BUTTONS:　　　　(wheeling round) Ah, there we are. (runs off D.L.)

(DOBBIN looks on again U.R. then enters and stealthily tip hoofs downstage to take the dandelion)

(AUDIENCE shout. DOBBIN starts back guiltily. BUTTONS runs on D.L.)

BUTTONS:　　　　(to AUDIENCE) Now don't you start. (sees DOBBIN) Oh, I see. I beg your pardon. Naughty, Dobbin.

(DOBBIN hangs head in shame)

BUTTONS: I'm saving that dandelion for Cinders. You wouldn't want to take it from Cinders, would you, Dobbin?

(DOBBIN nods head, then hastily corrects himself and shakes head)

BUTTONS: That's better. And why aren't you dressed yet? I told you to put your carriage on ages ago. Off you go and put it on right away.

(DOBBIN nods and exits D.R.)

BUTTONS: That's a good Dobbin. Ah, now for my cuppa. (picks up cup and saucer)

(Enter BARON D.L. in stockinged feet)

BARON: Ah, just what I need before we go.

(Takes the cup and drinks, while BUTTONS looks miserably at the saucer. BARON replaces cup on saucer)

Delicious, thank you, Buttons.

(BUTTONS turns cup upside down to see if there is a drop left. There isn't. He shrugs. BARON puts the bowler on)

Well, where are the girls? I'm ready.

BUTTONS: (offering BARON shoes) What about these?

BARON: Ah, yes, me dancing pumps. (putting them on) Ooh, they're ruination to my bunions.

(CINDERELLA enters U.L. with a muffler)

CINDERS: Father, don't go without your muffler. It's cold out tonight.

BARON: (winding it round his neck) Thank you, my dear. Now where are Tutti and Frutti? (calling to U.L.) Do hurry up, girls!

TUT & FRU: (off U.L.) Coming, papa.

(They enter U.L. with cloaks over their ball dresses and wearing very high wigs, which make them sway rather uncertainly)

TUTTI: How do we look, pa?

BARON: A bit top heavy. You'd better bring the carriage round quickly, Buttons.

BUTTONS: Righto. (gives a shrill whistle and calls to L) Dobbin!

(DOBBIN enters D.R. in the shafts of a small cart, which is very obviously an orange box on wheels. BUTTONS opens door U.R.)

BARON: I told you to bring it round, not in.

FRUTTI: And why haven't we got the ceremonial coach tonight?

BUTTONS: You mean the big orange box? The greengrocer wanted it back.

BARON: We'll just have to make do, girls. (sits in cart, completely filling it) In you get.

TUT & FRU: Where?

BARON: Oh, just squeeze in anywhere. Gee-up, Dobbin.

(DOBBIN neighs and exits, leaving cart behind. The shafts can have been held, through the skin, by the "front-legs")

BARON: (resignedly gets out of cart and into shafts) I don't know why we bother. This happens every time. Come on girls. (BARON exits)

CINDERS: Goodbye, father. Goodbye, Tutti, goodbye, Frutti, have a lovely time.

BUTTONS: And be careful you don't drink too much, girls.

TUT & FRU: Sauce!

(They turn to sweep majestically off R, but have to sink to their knees to get through the door. CINDERELLA moves to the window and waves to them)

CINDERS: Goodbye! Goodbye! ... They've gone now, I can't see them any more. Oh, Buttons, I do wish I'd been going with them.

BUTTONS: Well, I think it's jolly mean of them not to take you. But never mind, Cinders, I'll - er - I'll show you my Zoo if you like. (picks it up)

CINDERS: Oh yes, your lizards.

BUTTONS: Yes, the green ones and-

CINDERS: And the two white mice.

BUTTONS: That's right, and the -

CINDERS: The grey rat.

BUTTONS: Yes, and last of all -

CINDERS: The empty.

BUTTONS: I think I must have shown it to you before.

CINDERS: (sympathetically) Once or twice, Buttons.

BUTTONS: Yes, well anyway, it doesn't exactly fill in a whole evening, does it? We'd better do something else then. I know! We'll have a ball of our own.

CINDERS: With only the two of us, Buttons, and no ballroom?

BUTTONS: We'll have a huge make-believe ballroom, and huge make-believe people - I mean, lots of make-believe people. But first you must be dressed for it. Here's your cloak. (takes cloth from table and puts it round her shoulders. Noticing all the holes in it.) It's a sort of Aertex cloak this. (hands her the newspaper) And this is your fan. There, you look as pretty as a Princess. In fact, you shall be a Princess. And for that you need a coach. (turns the table upside down and puts the stool on it) Hey presto! One coach. I'll be the Coachman. (assuming a very aged voice) Your coach awaits you, your Highness.

CINDERS: Thank you, coachman.

BUTTONS: (helps CINDERELLA to sit on stool) Now, hold tight,
your Highness, here we go. (he sits in front of her on the table edge)
Get up there, you six white horses. Lovely night for a drive, isn't
it, your Highness.

CINDERS: Oh yes, so many stars and such a big, big moon.

BUTTONS: Lot of people about too. Listen to the way they're
cheering you.

CINDERS: So they are. (waves regally to the multitudes)

BUTTONS: And here's the Palace. Whoa back, there, whoa back!
I see the Prince is here to meet you. (runs round to help her out,
bows grandly and speaks in a very posh voice) Princess, may I
assist you from your carriage?

CINDERS: Thank you, Coachman.

BUTTONS: (in own voice) No, no, no, I'm the Prince now.

CINDERS: Oh, sorry. Thank you - er - Prince Buttonia.

BUTTONS: (in posh voice) This way, Princess, up the grand
staircase.

(They sink down then move round in a half-circle, rising step by
step to mime mounting the stairs)

Here's the ballroom. Isn't it huge?

CINDERS: Oh, enormous, and such a lot of people. Who's that
lady over there?

BUTTONS: The fat one with three chins?

CINDERS: No, the thin one with no chin.

BUTTONS: Ah, that. That is the Duchess of Dillwater. And the
gentleman with her is the Honourable Henry Hotspur.

CINDERS: One of the Northumberland Hotspurs?

BUTTONS: No, one of the Tottenham Hotspurs. May I have the
honour of this dance, Princess?

CINDERS: With pleasure, Prince.

(He bows low, she curtseys deeply and they take up a dancing position)

BUTTONS: (in own voice) Oh dear, I've just remembered something.

CINDERS: What?

BUTTONS: I can't dance.

CINDERS: Oh. Oh, well never mind, Buttons.

BUTTONS: Gosh, I'm sorry, Cinders. Look, let me - let me show
you round my Zoo again.

CINDERS: (shakes head) No, Buttons. (shivers) I'm feeling
chilly. Let's just sit by the fire.

BUTTONS: All right, I'll put these things back.

(Replaces stool by fire and CINDERELLA sits on it. He sets the table upright and gently takes the cloth from her shoulders and spreads it on the table, then removes the newspaper from her hand and puts that on table and kneels beside her. Pause)

(in low voice) Cinders.

CINDERS: Yes, Buttons?

BUTTONS: Feeling warmer now?

CINDERS: Yes, much warmer.

BUTTONS: (bringing orange out of pocket) Then p'raps you'd like a bit of this orange to cool you down.

CINDERS: Thank you, Buttons.

BUTTONS: I've been saving it up to share it with you. Which bit would you like? The inside bit or the outside bit?

CINDERS: The inside bit, I'm afraid.

BUTTONS: Funny, that's the bit I like, too. Well you can have it all, if you like.

CINDERS: Oh, thank you, Buttons. (starts eating orange)

BUTTONS: Cinders, there's something I want to tell you. Something I've wanted to tell you for a long time. And that is that I hope - I hope ...

CINDERS: Yes?

BUTTONS: I hope it's a nice orange.

CINDERS: Very nice.

BUTTONS: Good. They're always nicer when they're nice. But what I really wanted was to ask you if - if ...

CINDERS: Yes?

BUTTONS: If it's juicy?

CINDERS: Awfully juicy.

BUTTONS: I'm glad. They're more refreshing juicy. But what I was actually going to say was I wonder - I wonder...

CINDERS: Yes?

BUTTONS: I wonder if you'd give me a bit of orange? No, no, that's not what I meant to say at all. But it's so difficult somehow. You see -

MUSIC 28. "I LOVE YOU"

(Words and Music by John Crocker)

> When you're here,
> Oh so near,
> Things I want to say

BUTTONS: (continued)

> Jumble up,
> Tumble up,
> And then fly right away -
>
> For
>
> I love you,
> Oh yes I do;
> You're just ev'rything to me,
> And I wonder, could you please,
> Sometime or other love me?
> Oh, Cinders,
> If you could,
> Or if you would,
> Ev'ry single day I'd bless, yes,
> Joy and laughter,
> Happy ever after,
> If you'd only say, "Yes".

(Dance)

> If you could,
> Or if you would,
> Ev'ry single day I'd bless, yes,
> Joy and laughter,
> Happy ever after,
> If you'd only say
> Just one little word,
> Such a tiny word - Yes.

(EFFECT 11. Loud knocking at door U.R.)

Oh, why does somebody always interrupt?

(EFFECT 12. More knocking. He moves to door)

All right, all right, I'm coming. Of all the inconvenient times to call - (is about to open door, but jumps back) Ow, what am I doing? Supposing it's the Broker's Men back again?

CINDERS: I don't think they'd knock.

BUTTONS: Or burglars?

CINDERS: They wouldn't knock either.

BUTTONS: Or ghosties?

CINDERS: They can't knock. You're not frightened are you, Buttons?

BUTTONS: Oh no, but thought I'd just - er - just - open the door.

(He opens the door. MUSIC 29. The FAIRY GODMOTHER, still disguised, is outside. He slams door shut again)

Aah! Help! It's a witch! (runs and hides behind CINDERELLA) We'll all be spellbound in our beds!

CINDERS: Don't be silly, Buttons, let me see. (opens door)

FAIRY G: Good evening, child. May I come in?

CINDERS: Of course.

(FAIRY GODMOTHER enters. BUTTONS runs to fireplace and falls over stool)

BUTTONS: No, no! Ow, my poor shin!
            She is a witch!

CINDERS: She's not.

BUTTONS: She is!
            Else why's she got a witch's phiz?

CINDERS: Hush, Buttons, you'll drive her away.
            'Tis she whom I met yesterday;
            I help'd her find some kindling wood.

FAIRY G: And I've come as I said I should,
            To help thee when thy hopes are low,
            For are they not?

CINDERS: How did you know?

BUTTONS: 'Cos she's a witch.

FAIRY G: No, no, good lad,
            Just old and ugly, but not bad.
            Cinderella.

CINDERS: You know my name?

FAIRY G: E'er since into the world ye came
            I have been guardian of thy life,
            And known they troubles, woes and strife.
            But now much joy for thee I've plann'd.

CINDERS: Who are you? I don't understand.

FAIRY G: Then understanding I'll supply.

(BLACKOUT. FLASH. MUSIC 30. LIGHTS UP. FAIRY GODMOTHER revealed in Fairy dress, holding wand)

            Thy Fairy Godmother am I.
            And nothing can my plans forestall,
            You shall, my child, go to the ball!

CINDERS: A Fairy! Is this truth or dream?
            Are things as wond'rous as they seem?

BUTTONS: Such a rapid transformation
            Takes from me all animation.

CINDERS: But to the ball how can I go?
            I have no dress to wear -

FAIRY G: I know.
            My magic art shall that provide
            And footmen, coach and pair beside.
                    (to BUTTONS)
            But for these things, thy aid I'll need.
            Thou hast some pets.

BUTTONS: Oh yes, indeed.
I'll show you them. Wait half a trice.
(Fetches Zoo)
Now here are -

FAIRY G: Lizards.

BUTTONS: Yes, and -

FAIRY G: Mice.

BUTTONS: That's right, and last of all -

FAIRY G: One rat.

BUTTONS: You cheat, you read it. Well, that's that.
(He starts to take them back)

FAIRY G: Nay, leave them and bring one thing more,
That pumpkin.

BUTTONS: What, this 'ere? What for?
We're saving it for lunch tomorrow.
(brings it down staggering under weight of it)

FAIRY G: 'Tis in a worthy cause I borrow,
'Twill make the coach. The coachman, he. (Rat)
The lizards footmen twain shall be,
And these poor mice, now so afraid,
Two proud white horses shall be made.
Thus I'll create by mystic power
Cinderella's fairy dower!

(Waves wand. MUSIC 31. BLACKOUT. FLASH. BUTTONS and
CINDERELLA exit. Ballet and transformation follows. (This can be
done most easily - and effectively - in U. V. lighting, and the following
directions assume this.) Stage hands, covered in black costumes enter
during Blackout. U. V. lights up. FAIRY GODMOTHER points her
wand at mangle table and stool, which stagehands lift and carry off. She
points wand at fireplace. Stagehands slide truck off and the flat behind
to reveal wood wing. FAIRY GODMOTHER points wand at window wing,
which is swung round to show exterior on reverse side. She then
summons some of the CHORUS as Fairies. In the course of their dance
they take the prop lizards from the Zoo and place one in front of U. R.
door flat and one in front of U. L. door flat. At a wave of the FAIRY's
wand Stagehands slide these off L. & R. to reveal 2 of CHORUS as
FOOTMEN. FAIRIES then take prop rat from Zoo and place it in front
of C. flat. FAIRY waves wand and it is slid away to reveal one of
CHORUS as the COACHMAN. FAIRIES at end of Ballet carry off pumpkin and the prop mice and are followed by COACHMAN. FAIRY
GODMOTHER waves wand again, BLACKOUT U. V. and fade stage-
lighting up to suggest a fine moonlit night. She crosses and leads on
CINDERELLA in a beautiful ball dress and BUTTONS in a smart
buttons suit. FOOTMEN bow to CINDERELLA. FAIRY then waves
her wand and points with it to L. or R. as convenient, and the illuminated
coach enters drawn by ponies, (or CHORUS representing them), with

the COACHMAN. CINDERELLA is handed into the coach by the
FOOTMEN, who then take their places at the back of the coach.
MUSIC 32.)

FAIRY G: (to BUTTONS)
                     Now you, good lad, must go before
                     And tell the footmen at the door
                     To announce the Princess Crystal.

BUTTONS: I'll be off like shot from pistol!

(BUTTONS runs off L.)

FAIRY G: Sweet Cinderella, ere you go
                     One word of caution I'll bestow.
                     Be happy and enjoy the ball
                     Until the midnight hour doth fall.
                     At one second past that hour
                     Will the magic lose its power;
                     Coach and Coachman gone will be,
                     Thy dress but rags for all to see.
                     So till the time of twelve has struck
                     I wish thee joy and all good luck!

                     CURTAIN. CURTAIN UP.

             Coachman, away!

(The COACHMAN cracks his whip and the coach begins to move off)

CURTAIN

<u>MUSIC 33.</u> ENTR'ACTE

PART TWO

Scene Eight. THE PALACE BALLROOM

(Rostrum at back with steps down in C. Balustrade along back of
rostrum with a large clock with movable hands in C Wings L.& R.)

(CHORUS, as Ladies and Gentlemen of the Court, and DANDINI and
MISS MUFFET discovered)

<u>MUSIC 34.</u> "MINUET"

(Words and Music by John Crocker)

ALL: With such grace and distinction our measure we
                                                        tread
                A point of the foot and a turn of the head

GIRLS: A bow from the gentlemen to each lady fair,

BOYS: Who answer with curtsey as low as they dare.

DAN & MUFF: As we dance so sedately our carriage so staid
                We move round the room in a graceful parade.

DANDINI: To music so elegant our feet tap the beat.

MUFFET: No trace on our faces of feeling the heat.

                We give to our partners an occasional glance,
                A lift of the brows that we know will entrance.

DANDINI: Our hearts beat the faster when we catch their
                                                        eyes.
                We know the true feelings such coy looks disguise.

ALL: So with grace and distinction our measure we
                                                        tread,
                A point of the foot and a turn of the head.
                A bow from the gentlemen to each lady fair,
                Who answer with curtsey as low as they dare.

(ALL bow and curtsey to each other, DANDINI and MISS MUFFET exit
L. MUSIC 35. RAG, TAG and BOBTAIL, as Flunkeys, enter R. on
rostrum and stop in C. BOBTAIL steps forward, clears his throat im-
portantly and opens his mouth to speak, but no sound comes out. RAG
and TAG wait for a moment, their hands cupped to their ears, then
step forward)

RAG: What do you think you're doing?

BOBTAIL: I'm announcing.

TAG: I can't hear anything.

BOBTAIL: It's a silent announcement. I've forgotten who's coming.

        (TAG starts tic-tacking to off R.)

RAG: Oh, you're hopeless. (sees TAG) And what are you
playing at?

TAG: I'm helping. I'm tic-tacking to the flunkey down the passage to ask him who's coming.

RAG: What's he reply?

TAG: I don't know. He's not there.

(Enter the KING R. on rostrum. He has a beard and wears a large crown)

KING: Now, now, haven't you announced me yet?

RAG: I don't think so. Who are you?

BOBTAIL: It's him! The bloke I forgot was coming.

RAG: Oh, good. Who is he?

BOBTAIL: I can't remember.

KING: Well, what do you think I'm wearing this great heavy thing on me nut for? I'm the King, of course. Announce me immediately.

BOBTAIL: All right. (announcing) His Majesty King Ofcourse.

KING: No, no, no. You just say - His Majesty the King - not of course.

BOBTAIL: Beg pardon. (announcing) His Majesty King Notofcourse.

KING: NO. (to TAG) Look, you try. I'm just the King, right?

TAG: I see. (announcing) His Majesty King Right.

KING: WRONG!

TAG: Oh. (announcing) His Majesty King Wrong.

KING: No, no, no, NO, NO. For the last time, I'm just the King, that's all.

R, T & B: Ah! (announcing) His Majesty King Thatsall.

KING: Oh well, I suppose that'll have to do. (descends steps) Good evening, my people.

(CHORUS bow and curtsey)

CHORUS: Good evening, your Majesty.

KING: I trust you are all enjoying the ball?

CHORUS: Yes, your majesty.

KING: Splendid, then to add to your enjoyment I shall now sing to you.

(CHORUS look dismayed and back out L, and R. as quickly as possible)

KING: Now, why does that happen every time I say I'm going to sing? Dirty rotten lot. No respect for royalty. (turns to RAG, TAG and BOBTAIL) Never mind, I'll sing to you three instead.

RAG: Well, - er - I think we ought to see if any more guests have arrived, your Kingship. (sotto voce) Scarper.

(RAG, TAG and BOBTAIL run off L. on rostrum)

KING: (sighs) I'll never become a teenage discovery at this rate.

(Enter DANDINI L.)

DANDINI: (bowing) Your Majesty.

KING: Ah, Dandini, how fortunate you've turned up. I'm just about to sing.

DANDINI: (backing away) Oh no, your Majesty.

KING: (grabbing him) It's no trouble, Dandini. I've chosen a little number entitled, "It's A Long Worm That Catches The Early Bird Without Turning". (to CONDUCTOR) Thank you, Maestro. Maestro, come out from under that piano. Very well. I shall sing an unaccompanied chant entitled, "Somewhere Over The Silver Lining Is My Little Grey Home In The Wet". (brings hand up as if holding music) Oh blow, I've forgotten my music. Don't go away. I'll be back. (hurries off R.)

DANDINI: In that case I'll go and hide his music before he finds it.

(Hurries off R. RAG peers on L, on rostrum)

RAG: All clear.

(RAG, TAG and BOBTAIL re-enter on rostrum)

Now, carry on and announce the Hardups.

TAG & BOB: (announcing) The Hardups.

RAG: No, no, no. You've got to announce 'em separately like this. (announcing) His Lordship the Baron Hardup, the Honourable Miss Tutti Hardup and the Dishonourable Miss Frutti Hardup.

TAG & BOB: Old Uncle Tom Cobleigh and all, Old -

RAG: Shurrup!

TAG: Well, anyway, where are they after all that?

RAG: I dunno.

TAG: I always said the Hardups were a lot of nobodies.

(TUTTI and FRUTTI enter at R. back of auditorium, and move down R. aisle towards front)

TUTTI: Are you sure this is it, Frutti? It seems awfully dark for a ballroom.

(HOUSELIGHTS UP)

Ah, that's better. Thank you.

FRUTTI: Ooh, what a lot of wallflowers there are at this dance. Rows and rows of 'em.

BOBTAIL: There they are.

RAG: Oi! You're supposed to be up here, not down there.

FRUTTI: Well, we're just coming up there. (stops and moves back up aisle) Wait a minute, where's pa got to?

(DOBBIN runs on at L-back of Auditorium, neighing excitedly)

BARON: (off) Dobbin, come back, come back! (runs on chasing DOBBIN) Dobbin, this is not the stable.

TUTTI: I don't know, there are a lot of stalls here.

(DOBBIN moves along transverse aisle, being friendly with the AUDIENCE)

BARON: Stop making idiotic jokes and help me to catch Dobbin.

TUTTI: All right. (in heavy whisper) We'll creep up on him and take him unaware.

FRUTTI: (in heavy whisper) Take his underwear?

TUTTI: (in a shouted whisper) UNAWARES!

FRUTTI: Oh.

(TUTTI creeps up R.aisle, FRUTTI down it and BARON along transverse while DOBBIN ambles unconcernedly to the end of it)

BARON: Pounce!

(They pounce at DOBBIN who darts through exit at R.of Auditorium and they only succeed in catching each other)

Oh dear. Goodness knows where he'll get to now.

RAG: When you three have finished playing ring-a-ring-a-roses, perhaps you'd care to join us.

(They pick themselves up and move down R.aisle to climb up catwalk)

TUTTI: That's enough from you, my man. You just get on and announce us.

RAG: I did. I gave you a lovely announcement.

FRUTTI: Then give us another one.

RAG: Oh, all right, but you can only have a short one this time. (announcing) Baron Hardup -

TAG: And family.

(BARON, TUTTI and FRUTTI are now onstage. HOUSE LIGHTS OUT. They are knocked flat by the CHORUS who run on screaming from L, chased by DOBBIN neighing exultantly)

BOBTAIL: And horse.

(BARON, TUTTI and FRUTTI pick themselves up)

TUTTI: Oh, do take Dobbin to the stables, pa, he'll ruin our chances with the Prince.

BARON: Why? The Prince won't want to dance with him. Still, come on, good horse. (pulls at DOBBIN's head)

(DOBBIN shakes head and refuses to budge)

TUTTI: (pushing from behind) Go on, nice gee-gee.

BARON: It's no good. He won't budge.

FRUTTI: (crossing to R.) Leave him to me. I'll get him moving.

(She crouches down with head bent forward. Drum roll starts as she works herself up to run and continues as she hurtles herself across the stage. DOBBIN casually turns his head to watch. Just as she leaps to butt him in the behind, DOBBIN neatly sidesteps upstage so that she lands flat on her face beside him. With a toss of his head he walks calmly off L. with BARON)

TUTTI: Yes. Well, you did get him moving, dear.

(DANDINI enters R on rostrum)

DANDINI: Footmen, announce his Highness. (moves down to L. foot of steps)

CHORUS: The Prince! The Prince!

TUTTI: The Prince! Oh, Frutti, I'm all of a do-dither!

FRUTTI: Never mind that, help me up. (rises to her knees)

TUTTI: Certainly, dear. (firmly pushes FRUTTI down again with a foot)

RAG: My lords,

TAG: Ladies,

BOBTAIL: And gentlemen -

R, T & B: His Royal Highness, Prince Charming!

(MUSIC 36. Fanfare as the PRINCE enters R.on rostrum)

(CHORUS bow and curtsey. TUTTI curtseys still holding FRUTTI down with her foot. PRINCE bows in acknowledgement and descends steps to R.of DANDINI)

TUTTI: Ah, Princekins.

(Rushes towards DANDINI, FRUTTI lifts a foot as she does so making TUTTI trip and cannon into DANDINI. FRUTTI rises)

Oops, so sorry, Princekins. (throws a look of hatred at FRUTTI) I'm just falling over myself I'm so eager to meet you again. (pinches DANDINI's cheek playfully)

DANDINI: Ouch! My dear lady, I think you have made a mistake. This gentleman is the Prince.

TUT & FRU: Eh!

(PRINCE bows to them)

TUTTI: But I thought - I mean -

FRUTTI: (crossing to PRINCE) Princey, I must apologise for

FRUTTI: (continued) my sister. Of course, I knew you were the Prince, but Tutti is such a silly goose.

TUTTI: Oh, Frutti, how can you say that? I knew all along. I was just having a little game.

(Enter BARON L.)

PRINCE: Ah, Baron Hardup.

BARON: (bows) Your Highness.

PRINCE: Isn't your other daughter with you tonight, Baron?

BARON: Cinderella? I'm afraid not, your highness.

TUTTI: Yes, she said she couldn't be bothered to come.

PRINCE: (disappointed) Oh, I see.

BARON: I thought it was because you didn't -

TUT & FRU: SH!

BOBTAIL: Ladies and gentlemen,

TAG: The next dance will be -

RAG: A ladies excuse me.

PRI & DAN: In that case - Ladies, excuse me.

(They bow hurriedly and start to go. DANDINI gets away, but TUTTI grabs the PRINCE's arm and stops him. The CHORUS form themselves into couples. MUSIC 37)

TUTTI: Wait a minute, Princekins. Our dance, I think.

FRUTTI: (intercepting) No, it's ours.

CH GIRL: Excuse me.

PRINCE: Delighted, madam.

(The dance, a waltz, commences)

TUTTI: We've been diddled. Someone's swiped our perks!

FRUTTI: What downright imprudinence! We'll soon put a stop to that.

(They march over to the PRINCE and his partner and tap her on the shoulder)

TUT & FRU: Excuse us!

(They dance off with the PRINCE)

FRUTTI: Oh, what a pip of a dancer you are, Princey. No need to worry about you dancing on our feet.

PRINCE: (very gallantly) Ladies, I am too much under yours to be able to do that.

TUTTI: Flatterer! Heavenly music, isn't it?

PRINCE: Yes, but what a pity it doesn't seem to be able to keep in time with us.

FRUTTI: Don't you like our fox-trot?

PRINCE: Very much, but this is a waltz.

TUTTI: Oh, silly us! Is this better?

PRINCE: Yes, an excellent polka.

FRUTTI: Oh, goodie, and we can't even do a polka.

(Dance ends. PRINCE bows and tries to get away. DANDINI peers on D.L.)

PRINCE: Thank you, ladies.

TUTTI: I expect you'd like to have the next dance just with me, Princekins.

FRUTTI: Or would you rather sit it out - with me?

PRINCE: My dear ladies, until I have recovered from the - er - the supreme delights of the last dance, I assure you I shall dance with nobody. (hurries to R) Dandini!

(DANDINI enters with sheets of music. BARON joins TUTTI and FRUTTI and they chatter D.R.)

DANDINI: Yes, sir?

PRINCE: Dandini, don't ever leave my side again while those two are around.

DANDINI: Very well, sir.

(Enter KING R. DANDINI hurriedly puts music behind his back)

KING: Ah, my boy, have -

PRI & DAN: (bowing) Your Majesty.

KING: Oh, never mind all that bowing and scraping now. Have you seen my music? I can't find it anywhere.

PRINCE: No, father. Have you seen it, Dandini?

DANDINI: (airily innocent) Me? Oh, no, sir. (backs off D.L.)

KING: How very annoying. I wanted to find a song to celebrate your engagement.

PRINCE: But I'm not engaged yet, father.

KING: Well, do hurry up. The whole point of this ball is for you to choose a bride. And the whole point of you choosing a bride is for me to sing a song to celebrate it. Well, if I can't find my music, I'll just have to sing something from memory. Ah, I know the very one. A touching little ballad entitled, "Does Your Chewing Gum Lose Its Flavour On The Road To Mandalay?" (moving down) I'll try it over for you now. Ooh look, there's a dandelion growing in my palace. I think I'll take it.

(AUDIENCE shout, KING jumps back. BUTTONS runs on L, on rostrum)

BUTTONS: Ah-ah, naughty kingy.

KING: They shouted at me! In my own palace! (to AUDIENCE) I've a good mind to have the lot of you up for high treason. (stalks off D.R.)

(DANDINI looks on D.L. to see him go, then enters fully)

BARON: Buttons! What are you doing here?

RAG: Do you want to be announced?

BUTTONS: No, I've come to tell you to announce the Princess Crystal. (runs down steps)

RAG: My Lords,

TAG: Ladies,

BOBTAIL: And gentlemen -

R, T & B: The Princess Crystal!

(ALL turn. MUSIC 38. Fanfare. Enter CINDERELLA L. on rostrum. General gasp of astonishment. DANDINI moves forward and bows)

DANDINI: Gracious lady, allow me to present you to his Royal Highness, Prince Charming.

CINDERS: The Prince!

PRINCE: (bowing and kissing her hand) Yes, but now, most fair Princess, your devoted slave for evermore.

(EFFECT 13. Clock chimes and strikes eleven)

CINDERS: Not for ever, Prince. But for one hour only.

PRINCE: But one hour? With you 'twill be gone in a moment. Princess, I claim this dance and all your dances.

(MUSIC 39 starts. PRINCE bows. CINDERELLA curtseys and they begin to dance. CHORUS also, RAG, TAG and BOBTAIL exit L. on rostrum. DANDINI and BUTTONS exit R. BARON exits L, followed in high dudgeon by TUTTI and FRUTTI. CHORUS dance off L.& R)

Where have you come from, Princess? Why have we never met before? And yet -

CINDERS: And yet?

PRINCE: And yet in some way I feel as if we have met, as if I know you.

CINDERS: I feel as if I had met you before too. Maybe it was all just a dream.

PRINCE: Then we are so close that we share the same dreams.

"I'M IN LOVE WITH A DREAM" (Reprise)
(At end of number they exit R. TUTTI and FRUTTI enter L)

TUTTI: Well really, I can't think what the Prince sees in that girl.

FRUTTI: Neither can I. In fact, I've a good mind not to dance with him any more.

TUTTI: I've a good mind not to dance with anybody any more. I'm sick of men.

FRUTTI: So am I. Let's give them up.

TUTTI: All right. We will. For ever.

FRUTTI: For ever.

(DANDINI enters R. They take on seeing him and rush at him.)

He's mine!

(MISS MUFFET enters R.)

MUFFET: He's not - he's mine.

TUTTI: I think there must be some mistake. We were merely asking this gentleman the time.

FRUTTI: Exactly. We're not men chasers.

(They turn to sweep grandly off R, but 2 of the CHORUS MEN enter there and they wheel round to follow them, the pace of both pairs increasing to a run by the time they exit L.)

MUFFET: I don't think they were telling the truth.

DANDINI: Really? How very shocking.

MUFFET: I don't see why you're shocked. You haven't been telling the truth either. You said you were the Prince.

DANDINI: Ah, that was yesterday. Yesterday I was the Prince.

MUFFET: Who are you today, then?

DANDINI: Dandini.

MUFFET: And who will you be tomorrow?

DANDINI: Ah, who knows? How about the husband of Miss Muffet?

MUFFET: Oh. Oh, I don't know - I mean, perhaps - but then - well, you see - Oh dear, I think I'm a little confused.

DANDINI: Never mind. Come and have another dance. It might help to clear your mind.

MUFFET: Oh no. All that dancing round and round would get me more confused. Besides, it's rather frivolous. I don't quite approve of it.

DANDINI: Miss Muffet, you're a square, a dear, delightful square. And I know just the dance for a square.

MUFFET: What's that?

DANDINI: Why, a square dance, of course.

MUSIC 40. "SQUARE DANCE"

DANDINI: Let the fiddler start his fiddling,
          While we gather on the floor.
          Make the tempo nice and middling,
          Allegreto and no more.
          We would dance the whole night through,
          If you were us, so would you.
          Dancing rarely, fairly, squarely -
          That's what we're here for.

(This can be built up and other suitable numbers introduced, to make a production number involving as many of the cast as desired)

(At end of number all exit and KING enters D.L. with several sheets of music and some pieces of laundry)

KING: I've found it! Though I can't think how it got in the laundry box. Anyway, I shall now sing a little handkerchief entitled - eh? (holds up a handkerchief) There's been some hanky-panky here. I can't sing that. (throws it off) Instead I shall sing - (holds up a brassiere) No, I can't sing that either. It's a duet. (throws it off) I don't think there's much point in singing anyway. There's nobody here to sing to. Oh, bother, I'll go and eat. Where's that running buffet?

(He exits D.R. Enter L.a propelled table with a card in front on which is written "RUNNING BUFFET". TUTTI and FRUTTI chase on after it)

TUT & FRU: Hi! Come back! Come back!

(Enter BUTTONS R, wearing a policeman's helmet)

BUTTONS: (raising arms like a point-duty policeman) Halt!

(BUFFET knocks down BUTTONS and exits R)

That's the first time I've been buffeted by a buffet. (starts to rise)

(BUFFET returns from R.and knocks him down again)

FRUTTI: That's the second time then.

(BUFFET is going off R.as BARON enters there carrying traffic-lights switched to red. BUFFET continues past him and off R)

BARON: Officer, summons that buffet. It shot the lights.

(EFFECTS 14 & 15. Shot and glass crash off R)

BUTTONS: It's shot a chandelier now.

(RAG, TAG and BOBTAIL enter R.on rostrum, TAG and BOBTAIL carrying a rolled up mat. BUFFET enters R)

TUTTI: Stop that buffet!

RAG: Certainly.

(TAG and BOBTAIL unroll the mat which reveals itself as a zebra-crossing. BUFFET stops. RAG walks over crossing. BUFFET moves on and exits L. TAG and BOBTAIL roll up mat and throw it off)

TUTTI: You big sillies! You let it escape!

FRUTTI: So now you'd better come and help us catch it.

(ALL line up R. BUFFET enters L)

BARON: Forward!

(ALL advance on BUFFET.
BUFFET charges through them, scattering them and stops R.C.
They sort themselves out and dash R, but are unable to pull up in time
as BUFFET moves to C.and stops.
ALL hop in a step to L.
BUFFET moves correspondingly.
They try again with same result.
They pretend to be disinterested, then make a sudden rush towards
it, but just as they are about to reach it BUFFET bolts off L, leaving
them in a heap)

FRUTTI: Drat the thing. No wonder snacks are supposed to give
you indigestion.

(BUFFET returns L. DANDINI enters R.and puts out his hand as if at
a request stop. BUFFET stops and DANDINI picks up a sandwich.
BUFFET exits R. DANDINI crosses stage eating sandwich, watched in
open-mouthed astonishment by the others)

DANDINI: I hope you've had as much as you want to eat. (exit L)

TAG: (sighing) I knew we'd never catch it.

FRUTTI: What are we going to do then? I'm famished.

BARON: I think we'll just have to sing for our supper.

<u>MUSIC 41</u>. "A JOLLY GOOD FEED"

ALL: Now we would like a jolly good feed
'Cos we all feel very hungry.

RAG: And I consider that our very first need
Is a big bowl of soup kidney -
I'd lap-it, lap-it, lap-it, lap-it up with my soup
                                         spoon,
Empty folk are we,
But naught's so good as Christmas pud
To give you a full tummy!

TAG, TUT, FRU,
BOB, BAR, BUT: Now we would like a jolly good feed
'Cos we all feel very hungry.

TAG: And I consider that our very next need
Is a dish of fish kedgeree -
I'd fork-in, fork-in, fork-in, fork-in, fork in my
                                         fish dish,

RAG: Lap-it, lap-it, etc.

RAG & TAG: Empty folk are we, etc.

TUT, FRU, BOB, BAR & BUTTONS:	Now we would like a jolly good feed 'Cos we all feel very hungry.
TUTTI:	And I consider that our very next need Is a helping of roast turkey - I'd gobble, gobble, gobble, gobble, gob all my turkey.
TAG:	Fork-in, fork-in, etc.,
RAG:	Lap-it, lap-it, etc.
RAG, TAG, TUT:	Empty folk are we, etc.
FRU, BOB, BAR & BUTTONS:	Now we would like a jolly good feed 'Cos we all feel very hungry.
FRUTTI:	And I consider that our very next need Is a dollop of fruit jelly - I'd shiver-shimmer, shiver-shimmer shove in my jelly.
TUTTI:	Gobble, gobble, etc.,
TAG:	Fork-in, fork-in, etc.
RAG:	Lap-it, lap-it, etc.
RAG, TAG, TUT & FRU:	Empty folk are we, etc.
BOB, BAR & BUTTONS:	Now we would like a jolly good feed 'Cos we all feel very hungry.
BOBTAIL:	And I consider that our very next need Is a plate of cheese and biscuits -

(Music stops ALL turn and look at him)   Eee!

I'd munchie-crunchie, munchie-crunchie munch all
my biscuits.

FRUTTI:	Shiver-shimmer, etc.,
TUTTI:	Gobble, gobble, etc.,
TAG:	Fork-in, fork-in, etc.,
RAG:	Lap-it, lap-it, etc.
RAG, TAG, TUT FRU & BOB:	Empty folk are we, etc.
BARON & BUTTONS:	Now we would like a jolly good feed 'Cos we all feel very hungry.
BARON:	And I consider that our very next need Is a b'loon glass of French Brandy. I'd sniffie, sniffie, sniffie, sniffie sniff at my brandy
BOBTAIL:	Munchie-crunchie, etc.,

FRUTTI:	Shiver-shimmer, etc.,
TUTTI:	Gobble, gobble, etc.,
TAG:	Fork-in, fork-in, etc.,
RAG:	Lap-it, lap-it, etc.
RAG, TAG, TUT, FRU, BOB, BAR:	Empty folk are we, etc.
BUTTONS:	Now we have had a jolly good feed And we don't feel quite so hungry. So I consider that our very last need Is a nice cup of black coffee. I'd sip-it, sip-it, sip-it, sip-it in off my saucer.
BARON:	Sniffie, sniffie, etc.,
BOBTAIL:	Munchie, crunchie, etc.,
FRUTTI:	Shiver-shimmer, etc.,
TUTTI:	Gobble, gobble, etc.,
TAG:	Fork-in, fork-in, etc.,
RAG:	Lap-it, lap-it, etc.
ALL:	Full up folk are we, For naught's so good as singing of food To give you a full tummy!

(ALL exit R. CHORUS enter L.& R. KING enters L on rostrum with Music)

KING: Ah, people, good. I've got my music properly sorted out now, so for your especial delight, ladies and gentlemen, I will now sing a little number entitled -

(RAG, TAG and BOBTAIL enter R on rostrum, crossing in front of KING)

R. T. & B.: My lords, ladies and gentlemen, take your partners, please, for the last waltz.

KING: Oh, phooey!

(he throws down his music and stalks off L. on rostrum. MUSIC 42 PRINCE and CINDERELLA enter L)

CINDERS: Our time is nearly up, sweet Prince, I must leave soon.

PRINCE: Oh no, now that we have found each other we must never part again. Come, I will dance such ideas out of your head.

(PRINCE & CINDERELLA & CHORUS couples bow and curtsey to each other and begin dance. BUTTONS enters R, and looks wistfully at PRINCE & CINDERELLA. TUTTI & BARON enter dancing R, FRUTTI & KING L, & DANDINI & MISS MUFFET L.)

(EFFECT 16. The clock chimes the hour & begins to strike. On the first stroke - BLACKOUT. Crystal slipper is set at top of steps. LIGHTS UP a little. ALL have stopped dancing and there is a general buzz of excitement.)

PRINCE: Princess, where are you?

(CINDERELLA's double, in rags, is seen running up steps and disappearing L on rostrum. On last stroke of 12 - LIGHTS UP TO FULL)

She has gone! The Princess Crystal has gone! Dandini, she must be found!

DANDINI: But where, sir, where? She has never been seen before and we know not whence she came.

PRINCE: Yes, perhaps it was all some fairy enchantment.

DANDINI: (seeing slipper & seizing it) No, sir, look! She has left this crystal slipper behind.

PRINCE: Then find her we will! This slipper is very small - few feet can be so dainty. Dandini, issue this proclamation -

(MUSIC 43. "PROCLAMATION")

> Ev'ry lady throughout the land,
> Be she lowly or be she grand,
> By all the slipper must be tried,
> She whom it fits, I claim as bride!

(BLACKOUT)

Close traverse tabs. Fly in Scene 9 Frontcloth, if used)

Scene Nine - A FOREST GLADE

(Frontcloth or tabs. If cloth is used tabs to start)

(MUSIC 44. The BEAR is discovered asleep in C.)

FRUTTI: (off R.) Oh, don't lag behind so, everyone.

(BEAR sits up growling)

TUTTI: (off R.) Well, we're weak from lack of food.

(Traverse tabs open, but not fully. If cloth is not used, open tabs sufficiently to reveal a 6 ft.flat, suitably painted)

BUTTONS: (off R.) Yes, I'm jolly hungry.

(BEAR nods head vigorously, points to himself and rubs tummy, then runs to behind tabs R.)

(Enter R, FRUTTI, TUTTI, BUTTONS & BARON pulling the cart with DOBBIN sleeping peacefully in it)

BARON: And I'm jolly tired. Are you sure this is the right way, Frutti?

(During the following dialogue, BEAR creeps out from behind tabs and DOBBIN wakes. Seeing the BEAR he jumps out of the cart and runs off R. The BEAR gets into the cart)

FRUTTI: Of course it is. It's a short cut.

BUTTONS: Ah, that explains why we've had to walk so far.

BARON: Well, let's keep moving then.

(They all move L.)

Oh, Dobbin, you are a weight.

(BEAR growls)

TUTTI: Pa, I warned you against those radishes.

(FRUTTI, TUTTI & BUTTONS exit L.)

BARON: What's she talking about? That was Dobbin growling. Dobbin growling? He doesn't growl. (turns and sees BEAR) AAAHH! Help!

(BEAR jumps out of cart and BARON runs off L, then reappears without cart and stands in front of BEAR without seeing him)

Well, that's got rid of him.

(BEAR grabs him and pulls him behind tabs R)

BARON: Help! The forest's full of bears! Help!

(BEAR brings on matches and made up sticks for a fire, which he places C.and lights, then rubs his tummy)

BUTTONS: (singing off R) It's a long way to Tipperary, It's a long way to go.

(BEAR scuttles behind tabs R, and FRUTTI, TUTTI and BUTTONS enter R.)

BUTTONS: You know, I've a feeling we've been through this bit of the wood before.

FRUTTI: How could we have? Look, there's a fire. We haven't come across a fire before, have we?

TUTTI: Oh, good. We can warm ourselves up.

(BEAR comes out from tabs growling and pulls BUTTONS off there, keeping a paw over his mouth)

FRUTTI: No, I think there's a touch of thunder in the air. Better keep going.

(FRUTTI & TUTTI exit L.)

(BEAR brings on large salt and pepper pots and a huge knife, which he feels the edge of and rubs his tummy)

FRUTTI: (off R.) Come along, you others. We're nearly there now, just round this corner.

(BEAR runs off behind tabs. FRUTTI & TUTTI enter R.)

Well, round the next corner, then.

TUTTI: Are you sure this is the right way, Frutti? I feel as if we've just been walking round and round in circles. Look - there's that fire again.

FRUTTI: Eh? No, that's a different one. It's got salt and pepper pots beside it.

(BEAR comes out from tabs growling and pulls TUTTI off)

FRUTTI: Oh, just listen, Tutti - a brindled poppycock calling to its mate. (exits L)

(BEAR brings on a large cauldron, which he sets up over fire. Chucks the salt and pepper pots in and stirs them up with the knife, then rubs his tummy.)

FRUTTI: (off R.) Oh, you are a lot of loiterers, aren't you?

(BEAR runs behind tabs, taking knife. FRUTTI enters R)

Well, I never, here's another fire, dears. I wonder what's cooking? (sniffs at cauldron) I said, I wonder what's cooking? Well, do answer somebody. I might as well talk to myself as you lot.

(BEAR creeps from tabs to behind FRUTTI and growls)

FRUTTI: I can't understand a word you're saying, Pa. (touches (BEAR's arm) Oh, I didn't know you were wearing your fur wrap, Tutti.

(FRUTTI turns to R, BEAR slips behind her)

FRUTTI: Ow, where are you all? I've lost them!

(BEAR taps her on shoulder)

(to AUDIENCE) You know, I've got a sort of a feeling there's something behind me. Is there? ... There is? What? ... A bear? Oh no, really? I can hardly believe you. I'll look and see.

(Turns to L, BEAR moves with her)

Ooh, you're fibbing. There isn't a bear there. In fact, it's bare there. Oh, how droll! ... Well, all right, I'll look again all the way round.

(FRUTTI moves round in a circle anti-clockwise until she is facing AUDIENCE, with the BEAR keeping behind her)

You're just a lot of story-tellers, there's no bear anywhere ... No, there isn't. Well, I'll look just once more.

(She does a quick jump to L, BEAR does likewise, she jumps to front again, so does BEAR)

You're having me on ... Yes, you are.

(BEAR moves beside her)

(turning to BEAR) Aren't they?

(BEAR nods and growls)

There, you see, the bear agrees with me. (slow burn) Aaahhh!

(She starts to run, BEAR chases her, catches her and pulls her off behind tabs, despite her violent struggles. Returns with a large OXO cube which he topples into cauldron and exits behind tabs again, to push on at knife point BARON, in shirt socks and suspenders, BUTTONS in combinations with a lot of buttons down the front, and TUTTI and FRUTTI in their underwear. He leaves them and crosses to stir the cauldron)

TUTTI: Oh dear, whatever is it going to do with us?

(BEAR indicates them, then cauldron and rubs his tummy)

BARON: I'll give you one guess.

FRUTTI: I never thought I'd end up as a pot roast.

BARON: We must do something. Can't you charm bears, like you charm snakes?

BUTTONS: I think you can make 'em dance to music.

TUTTI: There, if only I'd thought to pop a piano in my undies.

BUTTONS: Well, I popped this tin whistle in mine. (produces a tin whistle)

TUTTI: Well done. What are you going to play? "Down In The Forest Something Stirred"?

FRUTTI: Or how about "The Teddy Bears Pic-Nic"?

BUTTONS: Oh, I don't know how to play it yet.

(BEAR feels the edge of the knife)

BARON: Now's your chance to learn, then. Play anything.

(BUTTONS blows a piercing shriek on the pipe. The others put their
fingers in their ears. BEAR runs and hides behind cauldron then
slowly peers over the top)

BUTTONS: Sorry.

BARON: Not at all, you're doing very well. What's a perforated
ear drum at a time like this? Try another piece from your repertoire.

(BUTTONS plays a very bad scale and BEAR throws knife into cauldron
indignantly and comes from behind it shaking his head violently)

TUTTI: I think he's going to start dancing.

BARON: Either that, or he's going to have an apoplectic fit.

(BEAR rushes forward and wrenches pipe from BUTTONS. ALL
shriek and cower away. The BEAR commences playing the pipe very
well and a glazed look comes into their eyes and they start to dance
in a trance-like way, which culminates in their all dancing into each
other and falling over)

BARON: I don't know about us charming him. He charmed us.
Still, if we keep dancing, we may be able to escape.

(They rise and start dancing again. BEAR is absorbed in his music
and does not notice that they are dancing off L, except TUTTI who has
become carried away again and is dancing the other way. The others
dance back and direct her steps so that she escapes off L. with them.

(BEAR finishes playing with a suitable flourish and turns to receive
some applause from his captives and finds they have deserted him.
Scratches head puzzled, looks around then rubs tummy sadly and
shrugs. Moves up to cauldron, throws the pipe into it and lifts it
off the fire; blows out the fire, puts that in cauldron and carries the
whole lot off R. Returns, his eye lights on the dandelion, rubs his
tummy hungrily and moves to pick it)

(AUDIENCE shout. BUTTONS runs on L)

BUTTONS: Thank you. Oh, you wicked bear. Trying to eat me
is one thing, but trying to eat my dandelion's more than I will up
with put, so there.

(BEAR growls menacingly)

And grrr to you.

(BEAR jumps back in fright)

Ooh. I'll try that again. Grrr.

(BEAR runs away with BUTTONS chasing him and "Grrr-ing", until BEAR gets on his knees holding out his front paws pleadingly)

BUTTONS: You know, I don't believe you're such a fierce bear, after all.

(BEAR shakes head miserably)

And I don't believe you really eat people either.

(BEAR shakes head)

What do you eat?

(BEAR buzzes)

Eh? Oh, I get it, honey.

(BEAR nods)

Why?

(BEAR growls a scale)

Ah, good for the singing voice, eh? You're very fond of music. Have you ever written any songs yourself?

(BEAR nods proudly, claps forepaws and the SONG SHEET comes down signed "A. BEAR")

Oh, isn't that clever? Could I try singing it?

(BEAR graciously gives his consent, and settles down at side of stage to listen)

BUTTONS: Thank you. (to CONDUCTOR) Could I have some music please, Charlie?

CONDUCTOR: Yes, of course.

MUSIC 45. "BIG BEAR, LITTLE BEAR"

BUTTONS: A great big bear got all dress'd up,
But pants he could not find.
He was most embarrass'd, I declare,
Until he met a little bear.
Now the great big bear walks down the road
With a little bear behind.

Yes, well that's a most unusual song, bear.

(BEAR is modestly pleased)

BUTTONS: I don't think we should keep a song like that to ourselves. I know, I'll surprise all those people out there and ask them to sing it, too. (to AUDIENCE) I say, I want all of you to sing this song. Yes, every one of you. Right, give them some music, Charlie.

(BUTTONS lets AUDIENCE sing for a little and then stops them)

Oh, dear me, no. That wasn't good enough, was it, Bear?

(BEAR shakes head vigorously)

BUTTONS: I want you <u>all</u> to sing. We'll try again. Thank you, Charlie. (leads AUDIENCE through song sheet) Ah, that was much better.

(BARON, TUTTI and FRUTTI enter at R.of Auditorium. HOUSELIGHTS UP)

TUTTI: Buttons, we've been looking for you all over the place.

FRUTTI: Yes, what are you doing?

BUTTONS: We're having a bit of a sing-song. You've arrived at just the right time. I was just going to ask some of the children to come up here and sing by themselves, so now you can help them up.

BARON: But what about old Bruin there?

BUTTONS: Oh, don't worry about him, he's really quite harmless.

(TUTTI, FRUTTI and BARON encourage the children up and help them over the catwalk. Ad lib singing with the children)

That was splendid, now you can go back to your Mums and Dads and while you're getting down, they can do a bit of work. Come on, just the grownups this time. Thank you, Charlie.

(TUTTI, FRUTTI and BARON help the children down while the adults sing. When the children are clear they join BUTTONS on the stage. HOUSE OUT)

Right, now you're all together again I want everybody to sing it just once more and as it's the last time really let yourselves go.

(Fly Song Sheet, close traverse tabs and frontcloth as they sing for the last time. BUTTONS, BARON, TUTTI and FRUTTI exit L., waving to AUDIENCE and BEAR. BEAR exits R.waving back to them)

<u>BLACKOUT</u>

(Open traverse tabs)

Scene Ten. THE MUSIC ROOM AT
HARDUP HALL

(Backcloth in front of rostrum, or flats, with comic pictures of famous composers painted on. Wings L.& R. Chair U.L.C. with false seat. Chair U.R.C. Music stand 1, D.L. Music stands 2, 3, 4 & 5 set apart from it in a line across C)

(CINDERELLA discovered dusting)

CINDERS: Goodness, I'll never have this room ready in time for the Glee Club meeting, but I don't seem to be able to think properly this morning. My mind's just a jumble of Fairies and coaches and Princes and - no, not Princes, just one Prince, my Prince. My Prince who danced with me all night. Oh, I feel so happy! And yet I shouldn't really; I shall probably never see him again; I should feel miserable, but somehow I just don't.

MUSIC 46. "SING A LITTLE SONG"

Though ev'ry sky is a dull shade of blue,
Though ev'ry dream simply will not come true,
Though ev'ryone seems to pick upon me -
    I sing a little song,
    And dance a little dance -
I'm happy as can be.

Though all the sweet things have turned into sour,
Though life drifts aimlessly hour after hour,
Look in my face and a smile will be seen -
    I sing a little song,
    And dance a little dance -
I'm happy as a Queen.

Clouds have silvery linings, so they say.
    Roads have odd ways of bending,
    Tales are happily ending.

When ev'ry sky is a dull shade of blue,
Here's the advice I would offer to you -
Wait for the sun coming after the rain;
    Just sing a little song,
    And dance a little dance,
And then you'll smile again.
    Just sing a little song,
    And dance a little dance -
    Just sing a little song,
    And dance a little dance
And then you'll smile again.

(TUTTI and FRUTTI enter R, carrying some music)

TUTTI: Now then, what's all this caterwarbling? You wait till the rest of the Glee Club arrive before you start singing.

FRUTTI: And while you're waiting you can put this music out.

II - 10 - 73

CINDERS: Yes, of course, Frutti. (starts putting music round on stands) Did you have a lovely time at the Ball?

TUT & FRU: No!

TUTTI: The whole evening was ruined by some silly young Princess.

FRUTTI: Princess? Huh! I don't believe she was a Princess at all.

CINDERS: What! I mean, why not?

FRUTTI: She was far too affected.

TUTTI: Yes, look at the way she arrived after everybody else and then suddenly disappeared in the middle of the last waltz.

FRUTTI: Never mind, I bet she didn't half look silly hopping home on one foot.

CINDERS: What do you mean?

FRUTTI: She left one of her crystal slippers behind.

(CINDERELLA gives a gasp and drops the music)

Ooh, my nerves! Cinderella, do be more careful.

CINDERS: Sorry, Frutti. (picks up music)

(BUTTONS looks on L)

BUTTONS: Some of the Glee Club members have arrived. Shall I show them in?

TUTTI: Yes, of course, we're waiting for them.

BUTTONS: Righto. Miss Muffet.

(MISS MUFFET enters L with a rolled up sheet of music and crosses to TUTTI and FRUTTI. BUTTONS exits L)

MUFFET: I'm afraid I'm a little late. I was delayed by the Prince to try on the slipper he found last night. He's calling at every house. I expect he'll be here soon.

(CINDERELLA gasps again and knocks over music stand 2)

TUTTI: Cinderella, you clumsy girl!

CINDERS: I am sorry, Tutti. (picks up stand)

FRUTTI: I really don't see why you have to racket around with those music stands. Nobody else does.

(BUTTONS enters L)

BUTTONS: Messrs Rag, Tag and Bobtail.

(RAG, TAG and BOBTAIL enter L. BUTTONS exits L)

RAG: Good morning, ladies. (bows to them and knocks over Music Stand 2) Oops, sorry. (steps to R.of it to pick it up and knocks down M.S.3.) Oh dear. (steps backwards over 3 and bumps into 4, swings round and trips over it, pushing down 5)

TAG: You missed one.

BOBTAIL: I'll do it for you. (pushes over M.S.1.)

RAG: Bobtail! I'm sorry, ladies.

FRUTTI: Not at all, it's the sort of thing that could happen to anybody.

TUTTI: Yes, we'll help you pick them up.

RAG: (rising) Thank you. Tag, Bobtail, give a hand too.

(BOBTAIL picks up M.S.1, TAG 2, FRUTTI 3, RAG 4, TUTTI 5. ALL standing to L of them except BOBTAIL who is behind his. They set them up and step back a pace so that FRUTTI knocks down M.S.2 RAG 3, TUTTI 4. At the same moment MISS MUFFET, who has been unrolling a sheet of music, drops it and bending to pick it up knocks into M.S.5. BOBTAIL looks at the fallen music stands, then at his own, shrugs and pushes it over)

RAG: Bobtail!

(Enter BUTTONS L)

BUTTONS: I suppose you're keeping them like that for singing low notes.

TUTTI: And I suppose you think that's funny. Well, you can just give Cinderella a hand to pick them up.

BUTTONS: Righto.

(RAG, TUTTI and FRUTTI move down from music stands. CINDERELLA picks up M.Ss 4 & 5, BUTTONS 2 & 3 and BOBTAIL 1)

(as he is doing so) By the way, there's a bloke outside who wants to join the Glee Club. He says he's a very keen singer.

TUTTI: What's his name?

BUTTONS: He said it was King.

(KING enters L, with a beard disguising his own and carrying a large pile of music)

KING: That's right. Mr. King. Well now. (plonks music on M.S.2 and knocks it over) Doesn't seem to be very strong. (tries M.S.3 with same effect) They're all a bit weak, aren't they? This'll be safer. (moves down L. chair and plonks music on seat, it falls through) Ah, this modern furniture's not like the old stuff, is it?

BUTTONS: (picking up M.Ss 2 & 3 again) Yes, he should make a good member.

FRUTTI: Buttons, be quiet. Your face seems familiar, Mr. King. Have we met before?

KING: Not in this beard.

TUTTI: Have you done much singing?

KING: That's rather a sore point. However, I shall now give you my rendering of a little glee entitled, "Down Among The Dead Men In My Alice Blue Gown".

TUTTI: We!l, I think you'd better wait till pa gets here.

FRUTTI: Yes, he's our conductor. (calling off R) Pa! Pa!

BARON: (off R) Yes, dear?

FRUTTI: Hurry up! We're waiting for you. You're the conductor this morning, remember?

BARON: (off R) Yes, just coming. (enters R. in a toy bus conductor's outfit) Any more fares, please? Hold very tight there.

FRUTTI: Oh, pa! Not a bus conductor, a musical conductor.

TUTTI: It's our Glee Club morning.

BARON: What? Oh, of course. Beg pardon. Pity though, I was looking forward to a game with this. Never mind. (crosses to M.S.1) Well now, let's sort ourselves out. Sopranos over there, please.

(He indicates M.S.5. CINDERELLA and MISS MUFFET move to it, also BOBTAIL)

No, sopranos, Bobtail. You're not soprano, you're baritone.

BOBTAIL: I'm not. I'm Bobtail.

BARON: I know, but you're also baritone. (pointing to TAG) He's baritone too.

TAG: How can I be, if he is?

BARON: Look, you're baritone, (pointing to BOBTAIL) he's baritone, (pointing to RAG) and he's baritone.

RAG: I am not. I've never even heard of this bloke, Barry Tone.

BARON: All right, you're all basso profundos, only get over here.

(Indicates M.S. 2 and they move behind it)

Now the contraltos next to you.

(TUTTI and FRUTTI move behind M.S.3)

And the tenor there.

(BUTTONS moves behind M.S.4)

Oh, we've got one over. Who's this bloke with two beards? He's rather like a chap I went to school with.

KING: Can't be me. I always went to school in three beards.

BARON: Oh no, it couldn't be you. This chap's the King now. Well, Mr. er -

KING: King.

BARON: Mr King? There's a coincidence. What do you sing?

KING: A little number entitled, "When Irish -

BARON: No, no, I meant what kind of voice have you got?

KING: I don't know. I've never managed to sing a song yet to find out.

BARON: Never mind. It'll be tidiest if you stand in the tenor section.

    (KING joins BUTTONS)

    Did you bring the tuning fork, Buttons?

BUTTONS: (crossing to him) No, I couldn't find the fork, so I brought a spoon instead. (gives spoon to BARON and moves back)

BARON: Oh well, we'll have to make do then. (strikes spoon on Music stand) H'm this spoon's a bit sharp.

FRUTTI: Don't be silly, pa. Whoever heard of a sharp spoon?

BARON: (strikes spoon again) Now it's flat.

FRUTTI: I don't wonder, you knocking it about so much.

BARON: (strikes spoon again) Ah, that's better. There's the note.

TUTTI: What is it?

BARON: B natural.

TUTTI: I am being natural.

BARON: I shall ignore that. Now, I'd like some scales.

RAG: Well, that's a bit of luck. I brought some with me. (produces some scales)

BARON: Not weighing scales. The other kind.

TAG: Here you are then, but you'll have to scrape 'em off yourself. (produces prop fish)

BARON: Singing scales! Now, sing. (bangs spoon again)

    (DOBBIN neighs off R)

BARON: Was that you, Mr King?

KING: Certainly not.

    (DOBBIN enters R. and neighs again)

BARON: Dobbin, what are you doing here?

BUTTONS: He thinks it's a horse opera.

    (DOBBIN nods and prepares to sing again)

BARON: Well, it isn't. Take him away, Buttons.

BUTTONS: Righto. Come on, Dobbin.

    (Leads off R.a very disappointed DOBBIN)

BARON: Now let us sing our scale, please.

FRUTTI: (huskily) I can't. I've lost my voice.

    (ALL get down and crawl about to look for it)

TUTTI: Well, it can't be far away, you've usually got plenty.

FRUTTI: (huskily) My right lung's gone completely.

TUTTI: What about the left one?

FRUTTI: (full voice) That's all right.

BARON: For the last time! (bangs spoon) Sing!

    (ALL rise and sing scale. BUTTONS returns. MISS MUFFET goes on up after the rest have finished)

MUFFET: I can't quite reach my top C.

BUTTONS: I see.

    (Brings on step-ladder from R., which MISS MUFFET climbs up and achieves a very high note, almost falling off steps with satisfaction)

    Timber!

    (MISS MUFFET jumps just in time. BUTTONS puts steps by R.side of pros arch and returns to M.S.)

BARON: And down again.

    (ALL come down scale. TAG keeps going down after the rest have finished, lowering himself to his knees and lying on ground)

    Very good. Now we'll try a song. Glee No. 44, please. "Baa Baa White Sheep."

MUFFET: A glee? That sounds rather frivolous. Can't we sing something more serious?

BARON: Very well. Dirge No. 44, "Baa Baa Black Sheep". Now, where's my baton? (produces baton from pocket, taps it on stand and raises it. It is hinged and falls over from middle)

TUTTI: It's wilted.

FRUTTI: It must have outgrown its strength, poor thing.

BARON: Oh well, I'll use this instead. (raises spoon) We start with the basso profundos. All ready?

R, T & B: Yes.

BARON: Here we go then. "Baa Baa Black Sheep".

(MUSIC 47. starts, BARON conducts with spoon)

R, T & B: Three blind mice,
                Three -

BARON: No, no, no. "Baa Baa Black Sheep".

R, T & B: Sorry. (they sort through their music)

RAG: This is it. (holds out a sheet of music)

TAG: But we can't sing that. It's printed upside down.

BOBTAIL: We could stand on our heads.

(BARON turns the music the right way ρ for them)

R, T & B: Oh.

BARON: Now, no mistakes this time, please.

MUSIC 48. "BAA BAA BLACK SHEEP" (In the manner of Handel)

ALL: Baa-baa, Black Sheep, have you any wool?
                Yes sir; yes sir, three bags full.
                Baa-baa, Black Sheep, have you any wool?
                Have you any wool?
                Any wool, any wool,
                Have you any wool?

                One for the master,
                One for the master,
                And one for the dame,
                And one for the little boy who lives down the lane.
                Who lives down the lane.

                Baa-baa, Black Sheep, have you any wool?
                Yes, sir; yes, sir, three bags full.
                Baa-baa, Black Sheep, have you any wool?
                Have you any wool?
                Any wool, any wool, any wool?
                Have you any, any wool?
                Have you any wool?

(During song KING is never allowed to sing. Every time he tries to come
in, he is either hushed by BARON or the others beat him to it. When this
happens he tears a piece off his music, till eventually he has only a little
scrap of paper left. He moves forward determined to sing it, but at
this point the number ends. He throws the scrap down and strides off
L,in a huff, while the others move forward to bow to their applause. As
they do so they knock over the music stands. They shrug and exit
BARON, RAG, TAG and BOBTAIL L: TUTTI, FRUTTI and MISS
MUFFET R)

BUTTONS: Well, I suppose we'd better tidy up.

(They tidy up music stands and music during following)

BUTTONS: I haven't seen you alone since the ball, Cinders. Did you get back all right?

CINDERS: Yes, but I only escaped just in time, before anybody recognised me.

BUTTONS: I know, and when you ran away, all your footmen and so on turned back into my animals. I had a terrible time trying to catch them with all the ladies screaming and jumping up on chairs. And I'm afraid we shan't have any lunch today. Somebody sat on the pumpkin and squashed it. Did you enjoy the ball, Cinders?

CINDERS: More than anything else I've ever known.

BUTTONS: I thought you must have done the way you danced with that Prince chap all night. Cinders - I don't suppose it's much use now, but do you remember, just before the Fairy arrived, I was telling you that I - I -

(EFFECT 17.   Bell rings off L.)

(calling off) I don't care who you are, you'll have to wait. - That I love you, Cinders. There isn't any chance you could love me, is there?

CINDERS: I do love you, Buttons, very much. But not in the way you mean.

BUTTONS: Oh. Not just a little bit?

(CINDERELLA shakes her head gently)

Not even if you tried awfully hard for about the next fifty years?

(CINDERELLA shakes her head even more gently)

Oh.

(EFFECT 18.   Bell rings again off L, more urgently)

DANDINI: (off L.) Open in the name of his Royal Highness.

CINDERS: Buttons, it must be the Prince.

(BARON rushes on L.)

BARON   Buttons, the Prince is at the door!

(TUTTI and FRUTTI run on R.)

TUT & FRU: The Prince is here!

TUTTI: Don't just stand there, Buttons!

FRUTTI: Let him in!

(EFFECT 19.   Bell rings again off L.)

TUT, FRU & BAR: Buttons! It's the Prince! Open the door!

BUTTONS: (very quietly) The Prince? Yes, I'll let him in.
(turns, gives CINDERELLA a little smile and exits L.)

TUTTI: Cinderella, come and tidy us up at once!

FRUTTI: And then get down to the kitchen and keep out of sight.

TUT & FRU: Hurry, girl, hurry!

(They drag CINDERELLA off R)

BARON: Dear me, it's so long since any royalty called I've forgotten the etiquette. Well, I'd better ask him to sit down, I suppose. (brings down L.chair) No, not on that one perhaps. (replaces it and brings down R. chair to C) That's better.

(BUTTONS enters L)

BUTTONS: His Royal Highness, the Prince.

(DANDINI enters, bearing a velvet cushion on which rests the slipper. PRINCE follows him on)

BARON: (bowing) Your Highness.

PRINCE: We are here on most urgent business, Baron. Are your daughters at home?

(TUTTI and FRUTTI run on R)

TUTTI: Princekins!)
FRUTTI: Princey!   ) (together)
)

PRINCE: (bows) Good morning, ladies. Proceed, Dandini.

DANDINI: His Highness has decreed that every lady must try on this slipper. She whom it fits shall be his bride.

FRUTTI: What a coincidence. I lost a slipper just like this one last night, didn't I, Tutti? (takes slipper)

TUTTI: No, but I did. (snatches it from her) So there's really no need for me to try it on. Princekins, I am yours.

DANDINI: (retrieving slipper) One minute, madam. This slipper must be fitted in his Highness's presence, so if you would just sit down.

(TUTTI sits on chair)

Thank you. Your left foot, please.

(TUTTI offers right foot)

No, your other left foot.

TUTTI: (trying to struggle into slipper) Anyone got a shoehorn? Nearly got it. That's it. It fits! It fits!

DANDINI: Except for the heel.

FRUTTI: Goody! Me next.

(Barges TUTTI off chair)

TUTTI: I don't know what you're in such a hurry for. If it won't fit me it certainly won't fit your great plates.

DANDINI: Your left foot, please.

(FRUTTI offers left foot and DANDINI fits slipper on it)

See, it fits. It fits!

PRINCE: What?   )
BARON: Good gracious!   )
BUTTONS: It's a swindle!   ) (Together)
TUTTI: It can't! It can't!   )

FRUTTI: (rising and moving to PRINCE, leaving behind false
    leg she has had concealed under her skirt) Princey, my Princey!

DANDINI: (holding up false leg) One moment, madam.

FRUTTI: Oh, blow!

DANDINI: I'm afraid we're out of luck again in this house, sir.

BUTTONS: But there's someone in this house who hasn't tried it on
    yet. Cinderella.

TUT, FRU, BAR: Cinderella!

PRINCE: Cinderella! Of course. I wonder, could she be?

FRUTTI: Ridiculous! She's a skivvy, not a Princess.

TUTTI: It couldn't possibly fit her.

BUTTONS: I bet it could, and I'm going to get her.

TUT & FRU: (grabbing hold of him) Oh no, you're not!

BUTTONS: Leggo!

PRINCE: Ladies! My decree includes everybody. As your Prince,
    I command you to let Master Buttons fetch Cinderella.

(They release BUTTONS)

BUTTONS: That's the stuff, Prince. Shan't be a jiffy. (running off
    R) Cinders! Cinders! (exit R)

TUTTI: I'm afraid it'll just be a waste of your time, Princekins.

BARON: No, I think she ought to be given her chance, girls.

(Enter BUTTONS R, pulling on CINDERELLA)

BUTTONS: Come on, Cinders, you're wanted on important business.

PRINCE: Cinderella.

CINDERS: Your Highness. (curtsies)

PRINCE: I want you to try on this little slipper. Will you?

BUTTONS: (pushing CINDERELLA into chair) Of course she will.

(PRINCE fits on slipper)

ALL:	The slipper fits!
PRINCE:	I have found her! I have found my lost Princess! Cinderella - Princess Crystal, will you marry me?
CINDERS:	With all my heart.
PRINCE:	(taking her in his arms) My Princess.
CINDERS:	My Prince.

(BUTTONS starts climbing steps by pros arch)

TUTTI:	Well I never, Cinderella a Princess.
FRUTTI:	Will that make us Princesses-in-law?
BARON:	Cinderella, my dear, I am very happy for you.
BUTTONS:	Cinders, this is for you. (plucks dandelion and comes down steps) As a - a wedding present. (gives it to her shyly) And I hope you'll be - I hope you'll <u>both</u> be very happy.
CINDERS:	Thank you, my very dear, Buttons. (kisses him)

(Rapture spreads over his face and he falls fainting into TUTTI and FRUTTI's arms)

And thank you, Fairy Godmother, wherever you are, for helping me to achieve this great happiness.

(FLASH. BLACKOUT. <u>MUSIC 49</u>. LIGHTS UP. TUTTI and FRUTTI try to hide behind chair letting BUTTONS fall. FAIRY GODMOTHER has appeared R.)

FAIRY G:	To me thy thanks ye need not tend,
	So blithely doth thy story end,
	Thou, Cinderella, pure and good,
	Hast gain'd thy right, as goodness should.
	So, but remains to wish thee well,
	And peal thy joyful wedding bell!

<u>MUSIC 50</u>. "WEDDING BELLS!"

(Words and Music by John Crocker)

ALL:	Wedding bells! Wedding bells!
	Hark with joy they ring.
	Wedding bells! Wedding bells!
	Be happy and sing.
	Happy the groom and the bride,
	Happy whate'er may betide,
	So join in their happiness
	Then will your cares be less,
	When you hear those bells,
	Wedding bells! Wedding bells!
	Hark! With joy they ring.
	Wedding bells! Wedding bells!
	Be happy and sing.

BLACKOUT (Close traverse tabs)

Scene Eleven. OLD BOYS REUNION

(Tabs)

(Wedding bell peal continues. BARON enters R)

BARON: Wedding bells, ah me! Fancy Cinderella marrying a
Prince. Old Beaver-face's lad. Beaver-face is what I used to call the
King, and he used to call me Toucher. We went to school together,
you see. Haven't seen him for years now. Not since I last got married
myself. He couldn't stand my second wife. Neither could I, come to
that. Anyway, now my daughter's going to marry his son. The only
trouble is, how can I pay for the reception? (feels in pocket) Tuppence
ha'penny. Well, I can't give them a slap-up do on that. Hm, who can
I touch for a neat lump of lolly?

(Enter KING L)

KING: Hullo, Toucher.

BARON: Beaver-face! I beg your pardon, your Majesty. Being
called Toucher carried me right back to my youth. Do you remember
how as a boy you were always wanting to sing? Ridiculous with a voice
like yours, of course. Still, I expect you've got over it now. I mean,
no grown man ... wait a minute, in the glee club, all those beards -
it was you, wasn't it?

KING: Yes.

BARON: Oh dear - well - er - you - er - you haven't changed
much, have you?

KING: I don't expect you have either. I bet at this very moment
you're wondering how you can touch me for a fiver.

BARON: Wrong. I'm wondering how I can touch you for five
hundred.

KING: Five hundred!

BARON: Well, it's your fault being royal. I don't want to let your
lad down at the wedding reception.

KING: All right, I'll tell you what I'll do, I'll pay for it -

BARON: Splendid!

KING: If you'll let me sing at the wedding.

BARON: Disastrous! You always did drive a hard bargain, Beaver-
face. All right, it's a deal.

(They shake hands)

I'll even give you a bonus. I'll let you sing now. After all, we were lads
together.

MUSIC 51. "LADS"

(Words and Music by John Crocker)

BOTH: Lads, lads, once we were lads:
Fags, fags, prefects and fags.
    Birds of a feather,
    We'd flock together
Playing at cricket and rugger and then -

KING: Grads, grads, two undergrads:
Bags, bags, in Oxford Bags.
    Far too much wining,
    Not enough dining
We were sent down, became men about town.

BARON: Cads, cads, girls call'd us cads:
Wags, wags, men call'd us wags.
    Billing and cooing,
    Flirting and wooing,
Woo'd once too often and found ourselves wed.

BOTH: Dads, dads, now we are Dads.

BARON: Rags, rags, riches to rags.

BOTH: But we must own up
We don't feel grown-up,
Older not wiser is all that we are.
Yes, older not wiser is all that we are -
At heart we're a couple of lads!

(They exit L, MUSIC 52. and the tabs open to reveal -)

Scene Twelve. THE ROYAL WEDDING
RECEPTION

(Fullset. Steps down in C.of rostrum. (Scene 8 could be used again)
CHORUS enter L. and R. of rostrum in pairs. Each pair meets in C, of
rostrum and comes D.C. to take their bow, then split and back away to
form diagonal lines L.& R. The principals follow a similar procedure,
forming diagonal lines in front of CHORUS. FAIRY GODMOTHER from
R, backing R: BEAR from L, backing L: KING from R, backing R:
MISS MUFFET from R, backing R and DANDINI from L, backing L:
DOBBIN from L, backing L: RAG and TAG from R.backing R.and
BOBTAIL from L, backing R: BARON from L, backing L: TUTTI
from R, backing L. and FRUTTI from L, backing L: BUTTONS from
R, backing R. MUSIC 53. Fanfare. ALL turn in as CINDERELLA
enters from R. and PRINCE from L..and meet in C, of rostrum)

ALL: Hurrah!

(PRINCE and CINDERELLA move D.C. to take their bow. Principals
move down into a straight line with them. CHORUS move up onto
rostrum)

PRINCE: Now Cinderella is my bride,
                 May like good fortune all betide.

CINDERS: But ere we bid goodbye to you,
                 We wish you well the New Year through.
                 And last, before you go your way,
                 We have our final tune to play.

MUSIC 54. "WEDDING BELLS" Reprise.

ALL: After the slipper did convince,
                 Cinderella won her Prince,
                 Now she's call'd Princess,
                 Theirs is the happiness -
                 Time to say farewell.
                 Goodbye now, goodbye now.
                 We must say adieu,
                 Goodbye now, goodbye now,
                 Goodbye to all of you,
                 Goodbye to all of you!

CURTAIN

Furniture and Property Plot

PART ONE

Set on stage throughout: Large flower pot in front of R. side of proscenium arch with dandelion flower to grow out of it.

Scene One

Set on stage: 2 benches under windows of Inn piece R.
Long handled broom by Inn door R.
Kindling wood sticks scattered L.

OFF L.

4 wheeled scooter with "L" plates and a hooter.	BUTTONS and BARON
Very battered dandelion with clock	BUTTONS
Large bundle of kindling wood	CINDERELLA

OFF R.

Bridle	DOBBIN
List	PRINCE
Few sticks of kindling wood and walking stick	FAIRY
Stirrup cup	MISS MUFFET

PERSONAL

BUTTONS	Fifty pence piece, notebook and pencil
BARON	Hunting crop

Scene Two

OFF R.

Large envelope with letter	BUTTONS

OFF L.

Book	MISS MUFFET

PERSONAL

RAG	Business card

Scene Three

Set on stage: 2 frying pans hanging beside fireplace L.
Prop poker on hearth L.
Sticks on hearth.
3 legged stool in front of hearth.
Besom broom by fireplace.
Prop mangle U. C. Prop iron and large bowl marked
        "EGGS" on top of mangle, with prop eggs
        and 1 ping pong ball.
Prop ham hanging R. of mangle.
2 saucepans hanging U. L.
Table C. On it prop fish and prop rolling pin.
(Table made in 2 pieces with one half sliding into
        other so it can be pulled apart).

OFF R.

3 invitation cards	PRINCE
2nd Table made in one piece to be substituted for other table	TUTTI and FRUTTI

OFF L.

Red end to be placed on poker when it is put in the fire.

OFF C.

Flat effigies of RAG and TAG to be pushed back through mangle.

Scene Four

If tabs are used notice in C. "FLUNKEYS WANTED APPLY PALACE"

OFF L.

Sheet	BUTTONS

OFF R.

Large packet marked "FERTILISER"
Large box, with sign on top "BUTTON'S ZOO", divided into 4 cages marked "Lizard", "Mice", "Rat" and "Empty" with appropriate prop animals in them   BUTTONS

Scene Five

Set on stage: Dressing table L.C. and on it; prop table mirror.
                 Hand mirror and hair brush.
                 Mop headed powder puff.
                 Prop cosmetic pots.
                 Coat hanger.
                 Set underneath: Large tin marked "BICARBONATE OF SODA".
                 Bottle of Guinness.
                 Frying pan and prop pancake.
                 Sheet of brown paper.
                 Toy pistol and a cannon.
                 Dressing table R.C. on it: prop table mirror and hand mirror.
                 Mophead powder puff.
                 Prop cosmetic pots.
                 Coat hanger.
Set underneath: Large tin marked "GUNPOWDER"
                 Flit syringe.
                 A roll on.
                 Toy machine gun.

OFF L.

Prop iron	BUTTONS
The scooter fitted with a bell and stirrup pump and bucket containing some water.	
Fireman's helmet	BUTTONS

Tin hat, bugle and white flag	BUTTONS

Various soft objects to fall from flies.

Scene Six

OFF L.

List and pencil	PRINCE

Scene Seven

Set on stage: The one piece table in C. covered by ragged cloth.
On table: newspaper, cup of tea, bowler hat,
      pair of shoes, tin of boot polish and brush
3 legged stool by fireplace as Scene Three
BUTTONS' zoo set above fireplace with large pumpkin
      hanging above it.

OFF L.

Muffler	CINDERELLA
Orange box cart on wheels with shafts	DOBBIN

OFF R.

Wand	FAIRY

PERSONAL

BUTTONS	Orange

Off (As desired)

Illuminated coach. This can be as elaborate as desired or a simple
profile cut-out mounted on a shallow frame - a depth of one foot
would be sufficient - running on four shepherd casters, with a bench
slat for Cinderella to sit on.

Whip.	COACHMAN

PART TWO

Scene Eight

OFF R.

Several sheets of music, handkerchief and	
brassiere	KING
Policeman's helmet	BUTTONS
Practical prop traffic lights switched to red	BARON
Zebra crossing mat	TAG and BOBTAIL

OFF L.

Sheets of music	DANDINI

Running Buffet: This is best worked by a person inside a framework
made as follows: A rectangular frame about 6' x 2'
and of average table height running on trolley wheels.
In the C., of the frame rises a structure representing
a large 3 tiered ice cake with gauze eye pieces on either

side. The table part is covered by a white cloth down to ground level and there is a large card on the front reading: "RUNNING BUFFET". Plates of sandwiches - (1 practical) etc. firmly attached to the table top.

Crystal slipper set at top of steps during Blackout.

Scene Nine

OFF R.

The Orange Box cart	FRUTTI, TUTTI, BUTTONS and BARON

Behind Tabs R.

Box of matches, made up camp fire with practical light	BEAR
Large salt and pepper pot, Knife	BEAR
Large cauldron hanging from tripod stand	BEAR
Large OXO cube	BEAR
Tin whistle	BUTTONS

Scene Ten

Set on stage: Chair U.L.C. with false seat
Chair U.R.C.
Music stand 1 D.L.
Music stands 2,3,4 and 5 set apart from it in a line
across C.
Duster

OFF R.

Sheet music	TUTTI and FRUTTI
Toy bus conductor's outfit and conductor's baton hinged to fall over in the middle	BARON
Stepladder	BUTTONS
False left leg	FRUTTI

OFF L.

Rolled up sheet of music	MISS MUFFET
Large pile of music	KING
Spoon	BUTTONS
Scales	RAG
Prop fish	TAG
Glass slipper on velvet cushion	DANDINI

Scene Eleven

PERSONAL

BARON	Coins.

EFFECTS PLOT

PART ONE

Scene Three

1	Door knock	**Off R**
2	Loud knocking	" "

Scene Five

3	Loud explosion (maroon)	**Off, as convenient**

Scene Six

4	Rattle of door handle	**Off, as convenient**
5	" " " "	" " " "
6	Handle turning squeakily	" " " "
7	Rattle of door handle	" " " "
8	Lock turning	" " " "
9	Door slam	" " " "
10	Squeaky hinge	" " " "

Scene Seven

11	Loud knocking	**Off R**
12	" "	" "

PART TWO

Scene Eight

13	Clock chiming and striking eleven, (set of chimes)	**Off, as convenient**
14	Pistol shot	**Off R**
15	Glass crash (bucket of broken glass flung into second bucket)	**Off R**
16	Clock chiming and striking twelve	**Off, as convenient**

Scene Ten

17	Clanging door bell	**Off L**
18	" " " , more urgent	" "
19	Clanging door bell, very urgent	" "

MUSIC PLOT

PART ONE

1   Overture

Scene One

2	Opening Chorus	Dandini and Chorus
3	Miss Muffet's entrance music	Orch.
4	Prince's entrance music	"
5	"I'LL FIND LOVE"	Prince
6	Baron and Buttons' entrance music	Orch.
7	Cinderella's entrance music	"
8	Comic dance	"
9	"I'LL HAVE TO DREAM UP SOMEBODY ELSE"	Cinderella
10	Dobbin and Ugly Sisters' entrance music	Orch.
11	"SONG WITHOUT REASON"	Ugly Sisters
12	Fairy Music	Orch.
13	"I'M IN LOVE WITH A DREAM"	Prince and Cinderella
14	"A-HUNTING LET US GO" (Continue, orchestra only, as link to next scene)	Ensemble

Scene Two

15	Reprise 10	Orch.
16	Broker's Men music	"
17	"LET'S DO NOWT!" (Continue, orchestra only, as link to next scene)	Broker's Men

Scene Three

18	Reprise 13	Orch.
19	"I WILL ALWAYS REMEMBER"	Cinderella and Prince
20	Chase music	Orch.
21	Reprise 20 as link to next scene	"

Scene Four

22	Broker's Men music, reprise 16	Orch.
23	"SING", (Continue, orchestra only, as link to next scene)	Buttons

Scene Five

24	Reprise 11 as link to next scene	Orch.

Scene Six

25	Broker's Men music, reprise 16	Orch.
26	"LOVE LETTERS", (Continue, orchestra only, as link to next scene)	Dandini and Miss Muffet

Scene Seven

27	Reprise 10	Orch.
28	"I LOVE YOU"	Buttons
29	Fairy Music, reprise 12	Orch.
30	Shimmer Music	"
31	Ballet	Fairy and Chorus
32	Finale background	Orch.
33	Entr'acte	

PART TWO

Scene Eight

34	"MINUET"	Dandini, Miss Muffet and Chorus
35	Broker's Men music, reprise 16	Orch.
36	Fanfare	"
37	Waltz for comic dance	"
38	Fanfare, reprise 36	"
39	"I'M IN LOVE WITH A DREAM", reprise 13	Prince and Cinderella
40	"SQUARE DANCE"	Ensemble
41	"A JOLLY GOOD FEED"	Broker's Men, Ugly Sisters, Baron and Buttons
42	"I'M IN LOVE WITH A DREAM", reprise 13	Orch.
43	"PROCLAMATION", (continue, orchestra only, as link to next scene)	Prince

Scene Nine

| 44 | Bear music | Orch. |
| 45 | "BIG BEAR, LITTLE BEAR" (Continue, orchestra only, as link to next scene) | Buttons and Audience |

Scene Ten

46	"SING A LITTLE SONG"	Cinderella
47	"BAA BAA BLACK SHEEP" Intro.	Orch.
48	"BAA BAA BLACK SHEEP"	Ensemble
49	Fairy Music, reprise 12	Orch.
50	"WEDDING BELLS", (continue, orchestra only, as link to next scene)	Ensemble

Scene Eleven

| 51 | "LADS" | Baron and King |
| 52 | "WEDDING BELLS", reprise 50, as link and continuing for walk-down. | Orch. |

Scene Twelve

| 53 | Fanfare, reprise 36 | Orch. |
| 54 | "WEDDING BELLS", reprise 50 | All. |